Maria writes with a winsome combination of personal experience and biblical exposition. Every woman and man needs to hear what it really means to be a "help meet" and to live joyfully in the strength of that calling. I believe that this book will encourage women to discover and use the gifts that the Holy Spirit has given them and I trust this will challenge the extra-biblical stereotypes that have often been imposed upon women—to the detriment of both women and men. I heartily recommend this book!

—Bill Taylor
Executive Director
Evangelical Free Church of Canada

In my work with victims of domestic abuse, I have seen Scripture weaponized against women countless times. So many Christian women have been told that their sole purpose in life is to serve their husbands and raise children—to the point that their roles in life supersede their relationship to God. Often, this sort of teaching stems directly back to how bible teachers and scholars have interpreted the phrase "help meet" in Genesis 2:18, or "ezer kenegdo" in Hebrew. In this thoughtful book, Maria Dyck untwists the many harmful ways this passage has been warped against women, but that's not all she does. In addition to correcting faulty interpretation of this passage, she goes on to reveal God's highest purpose for His daughters. I particularly love the last section of the book, in which she discusses the importance of women knowing their true identity in Him. I believe this book will be a healing balm to multitudes of hurting women who need to know that God not only loves them, but He delights in them, and has called them to help change the world as beloved disciples.

—Joy Forrest
Founder/Executive Director
Called to Peace Ministries

An author puts pen to paper to communicate something they've learned. When those learned truths are shared in the context of the author's own lived experience, they carry added value. I was privileged to be Maria's pastor for six years. My wife and I observed firsthand as she lived the truths she shares in this book; not perfectly (she'd be the first to say that), but faithfully. Day by day. Moment by moment. This book communicates the beauty, strength and grace God intended for this "help-meet" calling. You will be blessed by what you read. If you choose to embrace it, as the author has, the blessing won't stop with you.

—**Dan Carlaw**
Canadian Pacific District Superintendent
Evangelical Free Church of Canada

Ezer Kenegdo
עֵזֶר כְּנֶגְדּוֹ

TORN CURTAIN PUBLISHING
Wellington, New Zealand
www.torncurtainpublishing.com

© Copyright 2023 Maria Dyck. All rights reserved.

ISBN Softcover 978-0-6459696-3-4
ISBN EPub 978-0-6459696-4-1

No portion of this book may be reproduced, stored in a retrieval system or transmitted in any form or by any means—electronic, mechanical, photocopy, recording or otherwise—except for brief quotations in printed reviews or promotion, without prior written permission from the author.

All online references, including website links, are correct at the time of publication.

Unless otherwise noted, all scripture is taken from the New International Version®, NIV®. Copyright © 1973, 1978, 1984, 2011 by Biblica, Inc.™ Used by permission of Zondervan. All rights reserved worldwide.

Scripture quotations marked ESV are from The Holy Bible, English Standard Version®, copyright © 2001 by Crossway, a publishing ministry of Good News Publishers. Used by permission. All rights reserved.

Scripture quotations marked NKJV are taken from the New King James Version. Copyright © 1982 by Thomas Nelson. Used by permission. All rights reserved.

Scripture quotations marked KJV are taken from The Authorized (King James) Version. Rights in the Authorized Version in the United Kingdom are vested in the Crown. Reproduced by permission of the Crown's patentee, Cambridge University Press.

Cover art by Jeffrey McKee. Used with permission.

Typeset in Minion Pro, Myriad Pro, Berlin Sans, Orpheus Pro and Poppins.

Cataloging in Publishing Data:
   Title: Ezer Kenegdo: A deeper look at what it means for a woman to be a 'help meet'.
   Author: Maria Dyck
   Subjects: Christian living, women's interests, calling and vocation, family and relationships, Mennonite theology, discipleship, spiritual growth, personal growth, biblical studies.

Ezer Kenegdo

A DEEPER LOOK AT WHAT
IT MEANS FOR A WOMAN
TO BE A 'HELP MEET'

Maria Dyck

This book is dedicated to my sisters, Nita, Susie, and Kari, who have shown me what it means to be women of noble character and true ezer kenegdos.

Contents

INTRODUCTION		1
PART ONE:	FRUIT FROM A ROTTEN TREE	5
Chapter 1	Myths, Lies and Half-Truths	7
Chapter 2	Fruit of a Rotten Tree	17
Chapter 3	What is an 'Ezer Kenegdo'?	31
Chapter 4	An Identity for All Women	45
PART TWO:	SIX WOMEN FROM THE BIBLE AND HOW THEY WERE A 'HELP MEET'	55
Chapter 5	Sarah: It's Complicated	57
Chapter 6	Deborah: Leader Among Men	67
Chapter 7	Abigail: Woman of Integrity	75
Chapter 8	Sapphira: A Woman Lost	85
Chapter 9	Priscilla: A Woman of Faith	95
Chapter 10	Dorcas: A Woman Beloved	105
PART THREE:	LIVING YOUR CALLING AND LEAVING A LEGACY	117
Chapter 11	Our Identity Matters	119
Chapter 12	Our Calling Matters	129
Chapter 13	Our Legacy Matters	137
RECOMMENDED RESOURCES		147
ACKNOWLEDGEMENTS		149
ABOUT THE AUTHOR		151

Introduction

I FIDGETED IN MY CHAIR, moving my left hand carefully to keep it hidden from view. My grandma was visiting, and as we chatted over breakfast, I felt the weight of my engagement ring on my finger. It had only been there a few days—not enough for me to be accustomed to it yet. My grandma didn't know, and I was in no hurry to tell her.

My mom finally broached the subject.

"Did Maria tell you she got engaged?"

I felt my grandma's eyes drill down on me. Somewhat sheepishly, I lifted my hand onto the table, displaying the beautiful diamond on my finger.

For a moment, my grandma was silent. Then she said, "So you sold yourself, did ya?"

I understood my grandma's response; hers had been an abusive marriage. Many times, she had returned to her husband, only to leave again. The trauma of those years never left her, and carried on into the lives of her children. Our family was dysfunctional at best. It still carried the secrets, shame and scars of a broken generation.

Growing up in an Old Colony Mennonite family, you would be forgiven for assuming we led peaceful, quiet and holy lives, but the truth was far darker. As a young girl, I didn't understand the cultural and emotional undercurrents that permeated our daily life; I only knew that I didn't want to get married. Oh, don't misunderstand me—I wanted to be loved; I just didn't want to be a slave.

My view of marriage was shaped by my Mennonite aunts who lived in a constant cycle of babies, diapers, dishes. Wash, rinse, and repeat. Their life was one of quiet obedience and submission while serving coffee at the snap of a finger. I was not interested in being such a doormat for any man, no matter how wonderful he may or may not be. So, I resolved to never get married, or at least, *never* marry a Mennonite man!

But God had other plans for me. After finishing my music degree, I set off to the jungles for a year-long adventure teaching at a small Mennonite school in Central America. There I met Jim, and quickly realized I was going to cross off the first *'Never'* on my *'Never-to-do list'*. Jim grew up in a kinder, more gentle Mennonite home, which challenged my perception about Mennonite men, so when he asked me to marry him, I didn't hesitate.

I was at peace with my decision, but I dreaded having to tell Grandma.

～

Jim and I soon settled into life as newlyweds, but I thought of Grandma's words often. It grieved me to think of what she had endured in her marriage, and the bitterness it had caused. It pained me to think she had faced such brokenness and abuse, never experiencing a healthy or whole relationship as God intended.

I enjoyed my life with my new husband but I struggled to understand my position as his wife. I had read in Genesis 2:18 that God created Eve to be a 'help meet' for Adam but I had no idea what that meant. I only knew the struggle of being too assertive or too passive, too opinionated or too demure—it seemed I could never get the balance right!

The message I had absorbed from my childhood was that women were merely side characters in a movie which centered on the needs and desires of men. To reject this role was to place yourself in dangerous territory where angry women roamed, seeking the authority and power

INTRODUCTION

that God had exclusively set aside for men. I often felt I only had two choices: remain a doormat, or become a raging feminist. Stay sweet, or be a 'Jezebel'.

Were these my only options? Surely, there was an alternative! I wrestled with these extremes for years, trying to find a middle ground where I could respect my husband while being free to voice my thoughts and use my giftings.

Thankfully, my husband was much more relaxed about our gender roles, both in our home and within our church community. He valued my opinion more than I expected, and appreciated my input—a new and foreign experience for me. As a young couple, we ran a Bible study for the youth in our church. Even though I was a teacher, I assumed Jim would lead the Bible lessons—after all, women should be submissive, right? The problem was, every time Jim prepared to lead the lesson, he froze. He struggled with studying, and found leading stressful. He preferred serving coffee to the young people while having meaningful talks with them. I, however, loved teaching! I couldn't wait to sink my teeth into a text and create an engaging lesson.

For the longest time, we were conflicted about how to proceed. Eventually, as we prayed about it, Jim and I felt at peace to lean into the obvious areas of our gifting. From then on, I taught while he shepherded. We made a great, cohesive team. This experience was the beginning of learning to work together in our individual giftings for the benefit of each other, not worrying about whether they fit into our cultural 'norms'. I was me. Jim was Jim. And together, we accomplished a lot.

Twenty years later, we are more comfortable than ever with the different roles we continue to play in our marriage, our parenting, our church, and our community. I am the organizer, the planner, the dreamer. Jim brings the fun, the crazy, and the tools—just in case I break anything.

For many years, I had no words to describe the way in which Jim and I related to each other. We were simply partners, working together. Then one day, a question posed on social media caught my attention and opened the door to a new understanding.

"What is an *Ezer Kenegdo?*"

That was all it took for me to dive into this subject. I'm not sure anything excites me more than digging into God's Word to explore God's design and intention for His people, including women. Understanding what God had in mind for me . . . and for you . . . brings richness and meaning into our lives and allows us to step into the identity and calling He has for us.

So, what is an 'Ezer Kenegdo'?

Well, that my friend, is what we want to explore. I pray it will change your life the way it changed mine.

PART ONE

FRUIT FROM A ROTTEN TREE

1

Myths, Lies and Half-Truths

As a young girl, I wasn't very interested in marriage. Instead of dreaming about a husband and babies, I dreamt of being a fighter pilot or a spy—anything but the dreary world of cleaning house, baking and cooking, and being at the beck and call of a man.

These were my earliest ideas of marriage, no doubt influenced by what I witnessed in my home as a child. Having come from Old Colony Mennonite culture, my parents still lived with a very traditional sense of patriarchal authority. My father was the boss, and no one dared to question him.

There were many abusive aspects within our home, but I didn't realize it at the time because I was too busy trying to avoid my father's angry outbursts and survive his verbal abuse. I had a quick mind and a stubborn streak, but I learned to stay quiet and hidden, keeping my opinions to myself and waiting for the day I could find freedom.

For a Mennonite girl like me, the most respectable way to leave your parents' home was to get married. I had seen cousins jump into questionable marriages simply to escape their equally dysfunctional homes. While I needed rescuing, it became obvious as I approached the end of my teenage years that no prince was coming to save me. I was going to have to save myself.

Because leaving home as a single woman was considered dishonorable, I carefully planned every detail, knowing my father was sure to stop me if he found out I was leaving. I was twenty years old the day I finally found the courage to pack my bags and move out. As I suspected, my father was furious and demanded I return, but I had made up my mind and knew, no matter the cost, I needed to leave.

Over the next few years, I worked three jobs to pay for my schooling while I finished my music degree. After completing my degree, I found myself looking for adventure and a change of scenery. A friend mentioned that a small Mennonite village in Belize was looking to hire schoolteachers, so on a whim, I applied, and to my surprise, was hired.

Within a few months, I flew from my hometown in Canada to a small Mennonite village in Central America to begin my new adventure. I had just arrived in Blue Creek and met my new roommate when a guy in a blue Toyota pickup truck drove into the yard to take her to a youth gathering. As the truck door opened, out stepped a six-foot, dark-haired farmer with a moustache. *So that's what a Blue Creek boy looks like*, I mused. Fifteen months later, we were married and made our home right there in the village.

It was only after we were married that I began to wonder what it meant to be a 'good wife'. *What did submission look like? What did it mean to be a 'help meet'? Could I still have my own opinions? Could I honor God and still disagree with my husband? What should I do if my husband deliberately chose to sin?*

I had been taught to keep quiet. I had learned to stay hidden. But now, for the first time in my life, it felt safe to been seen and heard. My husband was not like my father, but I didn't know the difference between respect and reverence, submission and subjugation, service and slavery. It was all a jumbled mess of ideas containing some Scripture and a lot of cultural baggage.

At some point, my sister-in-law, who had grown up in Belize, handed me a book called *Created to Be His Help Meet* and suggested I read it. Resources were difficult to find in our little village in the jungle, so I eagerly accepted the book and dove into it. I was prepared to learn what it meant to be a good wife. However, I was not prepared for the message I was about to read. Several chapters in, I threw the book across the room in frustration. Instead of understanding what it meant to be a 'help meet', I felt attacked and belittled.

CREATED TO BE A 'HELP MEET"

While I couldn't put my finger on it at the time, I knew the message in Debi Pearl's book was incorrect. Her standards and interpretation of what it meant to be a 'help meet' were not only impossible to achieve but closely resembled my legalistic and oppressive childhood. I simply could not believe that a book endorsing abusive behavior reflected the heart of God. Even so, Debi's book haunted me throughout the years, its message always hovering in the background.

It wasn't until I came across the Hebrew term *'ezer kenegdo'* that I began to understand where the errors lay in Debi Pearl's book. I determined for the first time in my life to get to the root of this word 'help meet' which had long tormented me, and so began months of studying Scripture, talking to my pastors, and examining the selective verses in Debi's message.

What makes *Created to Be His Help Meet* difficult to critique is that among the lies and myths, the author makes valid points, but they are based on a theology which is Biblically flawed. The book is riddled with half-truths and cherry-picked verses which corrupt the definition of 'help meet'. It presents half of a story. Paints only part of a picture. At best, Debi's conclusions are short sighted. At worst, her advice is dangerous and potentially harmful, but in fundamental circles, and having sold over 500,000 copies, it's still the number one book on this subject. Google-search books on 'help meet', and there it is.

There are three main concepts in Debi Pearl's book which do little to explain what it means to be a 'help meet'. If we are going to gain a true and full understanding of this term, we need to examine these. One is a lie, the other is a half-truth, and the last is a myth.

The Lie: Being a Help Meet Is a Position of Submission

If you think being a 'help meet' equates to being submissive, you have either been grossly misinformed or lied to. It is simply not true! But this is exactly the position Debi takes in her book. She accomplishes this by quoting Scriptures about submission and authority, but on closer examination, the author simply uses the same nine references over and over again, giving the impression that the Bible is littered with such verses. One passage used throughout the book is Ephesians 5:22-24:

> *"Wives, submit yourselves to your own husbands as you do to the Lord. For the husband is the head of the wife as Christ is the head of the church, his body, of which he is the Savior. Now as the church submits to Christ, so also wives should submit to their husbands in everything."*

Debi Pearl uses these verses as a foundation to say, "God tells the wives to be subject to their husbands in everything; every decision, every move, every plan, and all everyday affairs."[1]

---

[1] Debi Pearl, *Created to Be His Help Meet,* No Greater Joy Ministries, Inc., 2014, p54

In a later chapter, her husband, Michael, gives specific examples of this, saying, "But first, know that a husband has authority to tell his wife what to wear, where to go, whom to talk to, how to spend her time, when to speak and when not to, even if he is unreasonable and insensitive."[2]

By the time the Pearls are done, you are left with the impression that you, as a wife, were created for your husband's pleasure only. To be a godly wife means you lay aside your thoughts, ideas, opinions, dreams and desires, and allow your husband to literally rule over you.

As we will discover, however, submission and being a 'help meet' are not remotely the same thing. In presenting her range of verses (often with no context), Debi Pearl conveniently omits other verses which present a more balanced view. Nevertheless, her view on submission, however popular, has caused a great deal of harm within Christian marriages and churches, and it's one we will discuss in greater detail in the next chapter.

The Half-Truth: Being a Help Meet Is a Position of Slavery and Service

At least three times, Debi Pearl quotes 1 Corinthians 11:8-9, ". . . but man did not come from woman, but woman from man; neither was man created for woman, but woman for man," implying that husbands were not created to serve their wives, but that God's design is the other way around. She explains:

> "God gave her [Eve] to Adam to be his helper, not his partner. She was designed to serve, not to be served, to assist, not to veto his decisions."[3] *(parentheses mine)*

---

[2] Debi Pearl, p260

[3] Debi Pearl, p96

It is true that we were created to serve, but what is lacking is the overall view of Scripture where God calls both women and men to serve each other. The Apostle Paul addresses this when he writes:

> "... for you were called to freedom, brothers. Only do not use your freedom as an opportunity for the flesh, but through love serve **one another**."
> Galatians 5:13, ESV (emphasis mine)

Since Paul was talking to the Galatian church in general, this encompasses both men and women. Paul does not command women alone to serve; instead he specifically uses the term 'brothers', calling them also to serve each other in love. Even Jesus stated that He came, "not to be served, but to serve and give his life as a ransom for many" (Matthew 20:28). The whole essence of the Christian life, therefore, is one of service: first to God and then to others.

So yes, we are called to service, but it's not a gender-specific command. It's for all brothers and sisters in Christ. As a wife, I serve my husband, not because I am *his* servant, but because I am *God's* servant, called to love and serve those within my sphere of relationships. As we will see in later chapters, serving one another is not confined to the context of marriage—it allows us to participate in a far greater vision and mission.

The Myth: Being a Help Meet Is for Married Women Only

Many Christian books, including *Created to Be His Help Meet,* use the term 'help meet' only in the context of marriage and for the benefit of wives. But this falls short of its original meaning. The truth is much richer and broader than we realize.

I believe God created every woman to be a 'help meet', and I hope by the time you have finished this book, you will agree that being a 'help meet' is a worthy identity and calling whether you are married, single, widowed, divorced, motherless, a teenager, or a little girl. God created women with a unique and particular calling, and this includes all women, regardless of their marital status.

If you are a woman, you are a 'help meet'. Period.

This is not an exclusive club for married women only, but a kingdom calling for every woman whether she is aware of it or not. This book is an invitation to begin exploring and understanding God's heart for you as a woman, and to realize He never intended the term to be used to hurt, degrade, belittle, or exclude you.

THE FRUIT OF ABUSIVE THEOLOGY

Debi Pearl's wrong conclusions regarding the definition of a 'help meet' is only one of a number of problematic issues within her book. Many of her practical suggestions for implementing her ideas border on abusive. For example, when a woman asks, "What should you do if your husband is cheating on you?" Debi's suggestion is:

> "You can hold out for repentance and most likely lose your husband, or you can 'court' your husband and win back his favor . . . make yourself more attractive than the secretary. You can win if you are willing to lose your pride . . . you must act as if you and the secretary are engaged in open competition for this man. Your husband is going to love what is lovely to him."[4]

The book also addresses the question, "What if your husband is an angry man?" by giving this advice from Michael Pearl, who contributed to the chapter on the husband's 'sphere of authority':

---

[4] Debi Pearl, p30

"Wives are to obey an unreasonable and surly husband, for they retain their headship until they cross the bright red line of criminal acts."[5]

In an online video, Michael Pearl instructs women that the way to get through to a violent husband is to ". . . make love to him. Get rid of his frustration. Make him happy."[6]

For the most part, Debi's book blames the destruction of a marriage on the wife. She describes what she calls 'a new breed of women', saying:

". . . (they are) independent, in charge, and stressed. They grow old early, trying futilely to care for unruly children whom no man wants to stepfather. They grow bitter as they watch eligible men look over their heads at girls much younger than themselves, who have no strings attached. And they grow fearful when they realize that the men who have shown interest in them are hiding perverted intents toward their cute little youngsters. Their kids are angry and often get into trouble. But all this was not your fault. No, it was your husband who committed adultery, your husband who was angry or got into porn, but he seems to have a life of ease now with plenty of money compared to your miserable condition . . . It all started when you were mad."[7]

What a harsh assumption! Yes, it's true that a woman may be at fault when her marriage implodes, but Debi's critique goes beyond calling women to account. Instead, it drips with condemnation and scorn—traits unbecoming of a woman of God.

---

[5] Debi Pearl, p261

[6] "Michael Pearl Censors the Internet", www.youtube.com/watch?v=0QntAr1OuzU&t=42s, December 12, 2011

[7] Debi Pearl, p71

MYTHS, LIES AND HALF-TRUTHS

Rather than encourage and exhort younger women as they navigate the challenges of married life, Debi belittles their struggles. When a young mother writes for help because she is feeling tired, discouraged, or overwhelmed with her home and children, Debi responds by asking her to take the 'Dumb Cluck Test':

> "Are you a dumb cluck? You asked me, 'What should I do?' You should get off your easy chair and learn to do a thing or two. Any good woman should be able to fix a screen door. Plumbing is not so hard either . . . Get off the couch."[8]

It is one thing to challenge women to grow and be accountable in areas that need changing. It's quite another to ruthlessly heap condemnation on one another in the name of Christ. This isn't God's way.

For those of us who grew up in an abusive environment, this sort of language and tone isn't shocking. We were conditioned to accept a demeaning and callous way of talking. But I have found as I've walked with Jesus, that He is far kinder and more gracious than many of those who claim to believe in Him. It is the kindness of God that leads us to repentance (Romans 2:4), not His contempt, though He would have every right to condemn us. If a holy and righteous God treats us with dignity and respect, how can we treat anyone less?

Sometimes, we cling to legalistic or traditional ways of thinking because we love boundaries and structures more than we love God. His boundaries were certainly designed for our good and our safety, but if we aren't careful, they can become idols. In the chapters ahead, I encourage you to rethink what it means to be a 'help meet'. *What roles are women given? What freedoms do we have? What does this identity mean for us? How do we walk in our calling?*

---

[8] Debi Pearl, p218

I hope you will find, as I did, that God's intentions towards us are gracious. As David wrote in Psalm 16:6, God's boundary lines fall in pleasant places and are far more liberating than we often allow. He longs for us to truly live as the women He created us to be.

2

Fruit of a Rotten Tree

As a young girl, I was molested. I have intentionally chosen not to reveal details of the abuse in this book; instead, I want to focus on the lasting effects of the abuse, which I spent years trying to understand. Sometimes the details in our stories are more distracting than helpful, but the journey to healing often looks the same. My experience was mild in comparison to others, but it was enough to traumatize me and distort my views on authority and submission.

The abuse taught me that men were not to be trusted and that to remain safe, I needed to withdraw behind walls of suspicion and cynicism. I learned to blend in with my surroundings and mute my voice so as not to bring attention to myself. Over time, I began to kill my own desires, distrust my gut, doubt my own experience. I struggled to believe that I was valued, worthy, and lovable. The effects of abuse of any kind are life-altering, devastating, and lingering—which is why Scripture speaks so strongly against it.

Sadly, I am not alone or unique. Within my Mennonite culture I have many friends who grew up in similar or worse situations, facing sexual or physical abuse at the hands of their fathers, brothers, or extended family. Despite its outward appearance, Mennonite culture has an abuse problem. Take into consideration the haunting story of mass sexual abuse that occurred in Bolivia in 2009, where multiple women were raped after being drugged with horse tranquilizers.[9] These events formed the basis of the movie, *Women Talking,* released in December 2022. While this was shocking to most Mennonites, the question everyone was asking was: *How did it happen in a culture that prides itself on being humble and pious?*

For several years, I hosted a podcast called *Mennonite Girls in a Modern World,* exploring the intersection of culture and faith from a Mennonite perspective. I learned so much more about my culture during that time, and came to realize there were two kinds of Mennonites: those who had enjoyed a safe and loving home and took pride in their culture, versus those who grew up in a harsh or abusive home and struggled with everything connected to Mennonite culture.

Those who love Mennonite culture are often offended when I suggest that we have an abuse problem. It's difficult for them to fathom the darkness when they have only walked in the light, but for those whose lives have been filled with pain and abuse, it's obvious. But Mennonites are not the only ones struggling with the proliferation of abuse within its communities and churches. Churches around the world are dealing with this issue daily, and the #MeToo movement has only exposed what many have suspected all along—the church is behaving very badly.

HOUSTON, WE HAVE A PROBLEM

To get a sense of how widespread the issue is, I spoke with Joy Forrest, founder and CEO of *Called to Peace Ministries,* to discuss the abuse of women within the North American church. Having escaped an

---

[9] Linda Pressly, "The rapes haunting a community that shuns the 21st Century", BBC News, May 16, 2019

abusive marriage herself, Joy was determined to help other women in similar situations.

Initially after her escape, Joy worked at a local women's shelter helping others as they came through the system. Many were Christians who attended church with their abusive husbands. On the flip side, many churches were reluctant to work with secular women's shelters, prompting Joy to begin a Christian ministry that would serve both abused women and the churches who desired to help. In their first year of ministry, *Called to Peace* interceded for three hundred women who sought help; this number has doubled each year since its beginning in 2016.

The numbers boggle my mind. According to the *US National Coalition Against Domestic Violence*, 1 in 4 women experience sexual violence, physical violence and/or stalking by an intimate partner during their lifetime.[10] *But surely not Christian women?* Sadly, yes.

Seeing the need in their local community, Dr. Steven Tracy and his wife, Celestia, began a faith-based not-for-profit organization called *Mending the Soul*. Together, they have developed a mentoring program and curriculum designed to bring truth and healing to those who have been abused. As a professor of theology and ethics at Phoenix Seminary, Dr. Tracy wrote the following:

> "In Maricopa County where I live, our community leaders conducted a survey of six hundred women to improve services to battered women. Roughly 85% of the women surveyed indicated that they were Christians; 57% attend church; 35% indicated they had experienced physical abuse in a past relationship; and yet only 7% felt they could confide in a church leader if they felt unsafe due to their partner's abuse. In another study of 1,000

---

[10] Jennifer L. Truman, Ph.D., and Rachel E. Morgan, Ph.D., BJS Statisticians, "Nonfatal Domestic Violence, 2003-2014", U.S. Department of Justice, April 2014

battered women, 67% indicated they attend church, one-third sought help from clergy, but of those who sought help, two-thirds said their church leaders were not helpful. Thus the evangelical church must begin to address this pressing problem."[11]

Eighty-five percent of Christian women indicated they were abused. That's an astonishing number! And only seven percent felt that the church was a safe enough place to seek help. This is deeply troubling. These numbers are shocking even without adding to the fact that abuse should not be happening *anywhere* where Christ is worshipped.

Where is the abuse coming from?

Professor Stevens answers this question by citing a study published in the *Journal for the Scientific Study of Religion*. The study showed that conservative men who attend church regularly are the least likely group to engage in domestic violence, while conservative Protestant men who are irregular church attendees are the most likely to batter their wives."[12]

Let's read that again: Conservative Protestant men who are *irregular* church attendees are the most likely to batter their wives.

In other words, men who know Scripture but fail to engage in Christian community are the most likely to abuse their wives and children. In contrast, men who know Scripture *and live in faithful Christian community* are among the safest men. There is something transformative about believers living in Christian community where they model humility and love, are taught God's Word, and are held accountable.

Old Colony Mennonites believe that cutting oneself off from the world is the best way to stay pure, but the level of abuse within their communities would suggest that isolation is *not* the best approach to godliness. In

---

[11] Steven R. Tracy, "Patriarch and Domestic Violence: Challenging Common Misconceptions", Journal of the Evangelical Theological Society 50/3, September 2007

[12] Ibid.

fact, I would argue it breeds violence and abuse because it isolates the victims (mostly women and children) from those who can help. It also leaves the men with little to no level of accountability.

The church within North America, despite all its resources, has a very big problem. In a place that should champion women being seen, heard, and valued, we are seeing abuse. This is not of God. At the root of every sin, there is often an abundance of lies, false teaching, and erroneous thinking. So we need to ask ourselves, *If abuse is the rotten fruit, what is the tree?*

THE TREE IS ROTTEN

My apple tree has not given me apples for four years. When we first moved onto our acreage, the tree was loaded with small, juicy, sweet apples. What a treat it was to grab an apple right off the tree and eat it. But over the years, the tree has been steadily producing less and less until this year, it produced none at all. I kept thinking it was bad luck or bad weather, but I've come to realize my tree is dying.

A dead tree can't produce fruit, neither can a rotten tree produce good fruit.

I love that God is a gardener, and He talks about the importance of being healthy in John 15. In this beautiful passage, Jesus warns that a branch which bears no fruit will be cut off, while a branch which bears much fruit will be pruned. *So how do we bear fruit?* By remaining in Christ. Apart from Him, we can bear no fruit at all!

But what about when a tree produces bad fruit?

If abuse is the fruit, we must examine the tree. Obviously, the tree is not healthy, because good fruit does not come from a rotten tree. If we want to understand where abuse comes from, we must examine what is being taught or caught in our churches. What is the church getting wrong?

Abuse is often complex, and there is not always a clear answer as to why it occurs. It can be the result of many factors in combination, but for the sake of this study, I want to look at several issues that I believe contribute to abuse.

ROTTEN THEOLOGY

We are what we think. What we think determines our actions. When we realize this, we understand that how a person acts is an indication of what they think. The two are related. So, when we see abuse happening in a Christian home or church, we have to look at the beliefs and convictions which are contributing to the issue.

I asked Joy Forrest to tell me, from her experience and observation, what characteristics were commonly shared among abusive men. Her response was that these men tend to have a great deal of pride, a strong sense of entitlement, and they are highly secretive, seemingly spiritual, and often service-driven to hide the fact that they are living a double life.

These men may come across as charming, attentive, respected by others, and able to quote Scripture. They may seem godly and serve on church boards, but in their innermost thoughts there is rot and decay. They do not honor women, and this in obvious in their actions. Men do not abuse women if they truly love and respect them.

Joy stated that, within her experience and ministry, a person's theological view about the relationship of men and women made little difference. Both complementarians and egalitarians could be abusers. This surprised me. I had assumed egalitarians would be more honorable towards women since their theology considers men and women as equal in every way. But obviously, if you are abusing women, your words hold little weight.

An abuser may say he values women, but when he mistreats them, his actions reveal his true thoughts. When you abuse women, you are screaming that they have no value, they deserve no dignity, they are beneath you, and that their needs don't matter. You believe they deserve to be treated accordingly and that you deserve better. This is an abuser's theology whether they admit it or not, and the fruit of this theology is abuse.

Secondly, I asked Joy what beliefs were common among abused women. Among her response was the idea that submission means blind obedience to your husband, that Scripture calls women to silence, and that divorce is the greatest sin you could commit. I want to briefly address these common misunderstandings.

Misunderstanding Submission

Misunderstanding submission is a common struggle for women in the church, particularly those who have been abused. If the abuser had a Christian background, it is very likely they used Scripture to verbally and spiritually abuse their victim, twisting the concept of submission to fit their agenda. An abuser needs his victims to be silent and passive, and using verses like Ephesians 5:22 ("Wives, submit to your own husbands as you do to the Lord") is a common tactic among abusive husbands. This is why a book like *Created to Be His Help Meet* can do so much damage. In the hands of an abuser, it becomes a weapon.

So what does it really mean to submit?

According to the Merriam-Webster dictionary, to submit means: *to yield oneself to the authority of another or to permit oneself to be subjected to something.* In other words, it's voluntary. If you are not submitting out of your own free will, then it's not true submission. If an abuser forces you to 'submit', it's actually called subjugation, which means: *to bring under control and governance.*

Many women have been taught the word 'submission' when the word 'subjugation' would more accurately describe their theology.

It's important to realize that submission is a term used among equals. As in, a wife submits to her husband willingly and as an equal. Anything beyond that is not true biblical submission. I appreciate Pastor Andy Holt's description of biblical submission:

> "The first thing we must understand is this: *biblical submission assumes equality.* Biblical submission assumes equality because it is a volitional act of humility in letting another lead. Like love, submission can never be forced upon or demanded of. *Submission is a gift freely given to another in humility, not the humiliation extracted by force from a weaker person.*"[13]

It's also interesting to note that while Mike and Debi Pearl frequently quote Ephesians 5:22-24, they conveniently omit verse twenty-one which says, "Submit to *one another* out of reverence for Christ."

Yes, the Bible calls wives to submit to their husbands, but the truth is much bigger than that. In Ephesians 5:21 it also calls husbands to submit to their wives. The placing of this verse is important because it sets the stage for how submission and respect are fleshed out within a marriage. Only after verse twenty-one do we read how a wife ought to submit, and how husbands should love their wives. Omitting this verse ignores an important aspect of Christian submission: we must first submit to God, then to each other.

It's important to read these texts in their full context, because if we fail to understand what it means to be submissive, and believe it is a position of subjugation and complete obedience, we run the risk of causing harm

---

[13] A.W. Holt, "Biblical Submission: What Is It? What Does It Look Like Today?", The Sometimes Preacher, February 25, 2016

to women. Helping men and women understand the true meaning of submission should be a priority for churches, not only to safeguard the men and women themselves but because healthy marriages are one of the building blocks of a healthy church. If your church isn't healthy, it may be that your marriages are suffering under harmful theology.

Misunderstanding 'Silence'

One of the most abused verses in Scripture was written by Paul as he gave instructions to Timothy for corporate worship: "Let a woman learn in silence with all submission. And I do not permit a woman to teach or to have authority over a man, but to be in silence." (1 Timothy 2:11-12, NKJV).

This verse has been used to cower women into silence in ways that God never intended, and in ways that do not bring Him honor. While there is much debate over what Paul's intentions were in writing this passage, there is no doubt that Paul considered women to be equal partners in the Gospel. Although this verse would make it appear that he did not value them, it's important to look at *all* of Paul's writing if we are to grasp his attitude towards women. For example, in 1 Corinthians 11:5, Paul assumes women will prophesy and pray in public. The command to be silent, therefore, needs to be aligned with other parts of Paul's teaching.

Abusers within the church specialize in taking a verse out of context and using it to control their victims, and this verse is a powerful weapon—particularly in the hands of a man who loves his position of authority. It has been wisely said, "A verse must be interpreted through the lens of Scripture, rather than Scripture interpreted through the lens of a verse." While Christians may not agree on the degree to which 1 Timothy 2:11-12 should be taken, the idea that women should be absolutely silent is absurd, and not in line at all with how the Apostle Paul operated.

The truth is, the Apostle Paul was a radical in his day, advocating for women's equality in a culture that treated women like chattel. In fact, if you study Christian history, you will find that wherever the message of the Gospel was preached, women were treated with more honor and dignity than in the surrounding culture. Author Sue Bohlin explains how this impacted marriage:

> "The biblical view of husbands and wives as equal partners caused a sea change in marriage as well. Christian women started marrying later, and they married men of their own choosing. This eroded the ancient practice of men marrying child brides against their will, often as young as eleven or twelve years old. The greater marital freedom that Christianity gave women eventually gained wide appeal. Today, a Western woman is not compelled to marry someone she does not want, nor can she legally be married as a child bride. But the practice continues in parts of the world where Christianity has little or no presence."[14]

One only has to look at the current headlines in Afghanistan to see what happens when men who believe in the subjugation and silencing of women are in control. Christianity should never resemble this. Our fruit should look different because we are rooted in the person of Jesus Christ. If women are silenced and subjugated, you can be sure it is not of Christ.

Misunderstanding Divorce

During my discussion with Joy Forrest, she shared that one of the most frequent and heartbreaking questions asked by the women she encounters in her program is, "Why does my pastor care more about my marriage than he does about my life?"

---

[14] Sue Bohlin, "Christianity: The Best Thing That Ever Happened to Women", Probe for Answers, November 27, 2005

God made marriage to be good and wonderful, but because of sin, all things on earth have become corrupted—including marriage. When abuse enters a marriage, it no longer honors God or is capable of completing the mission for which God designed it. Within the church we can be guilty of honoring or elevating a gift God has given, to the point where the gift is esteemed greater than the Giver and it becomes an idol.

If the church cares more about a marriage remaining intact than the safety and protection of victims, then we have lost the plot. We have lost sight of the forest for the trees. Yes, God hates divorce, but perhaps His hate is equally directed at what *causes* divorce, and not only at the divorce itself. By the time divorce occurs, there's already been multiple layers of sin, whether it is abuse, adultery, selfishness, or apathy. We should be more concerned about the sins that lead to divorce than the divorce itself. Deal with the roots before criticizing the fruit.

In cases of abuse, divorce may be the only option. As in all highly sensitive topics, it is important to get good counsel and surround yourself with trusted support. This is where a ministry like *Called to Peace* can play a vital role in helping victims find safety and healing.

Misunderstanding 'Help Meet'

There is one more issue we often misunderstand, and it is the concept of what it means to be a 'help meet'. It is the theme of this book, because in the hands of an abuser, this term can be used against a woman to coerce her into doing what he desires, while stripping her of her autonomy—all in the name of God. A man who understands what a help meet is will treat his wife with dignity, love, and respect. A woman who understands what a help meet is will see her own worth and value, and will embrace the calling and identity God has placed on her.

Truth really does set us free, and in the case of being a help meet, this is no exception. One of the saddest outcomes of living with abuse is the potential it has to warp your mind and change how you view God, and therefore, how you view yourself. The more we understand God and His heart for us, the more we will be able to guard our minds and live as He calls us to live.

UPROOT THE TREE

The church has a pivotal role and responsibility to be a source of truth and life for both the victim and abuser. For victims, the church needs to edify, strengthen, encourage and protect, while providing a safe place for them. For oppressors, it needs to speak truth, hold them accountable, and call them to repentance. Either way, the church must step in. Intended or not, the church has often been complicit in cases of abuse, either because the leadership failed to hold the abuser accountable, or by dismissing the hurt and severity of the abuse towards the victim.

Every pastor needs to be aware that the words they preach on a Sunday morning may be used by an abusive husband to oppress his wife. Every leader needs wisdom and discernment in dealing with abusive men who are often cunning and deceitful. Every member of the congregation needs to understand how to deal with abuse in a way that honors Christ. Some of the strongest words of condemnation in Scripture are reserved for those who oppress others. Jesus did not tolerate abusive behavior.

If we want to tackle the issue of abuse within our churches, we must look at our theology and practices to examine how they might harm rather than help victims. We need to be ready and willing to cut off any branch that isn't bearing fruit, and speak truth and life to those who are suffering under the weight of abuse.

There is much work to be done in this area, and my hope and prayer in writing this book is to shed light on how the phrase 'help meet' has been used to harm women, and how it instead offers a compelling glimpse into the heart of God and His design for them. Let's root ourselves in the truth of God's Word and take a fresh look at the calling of Eve in the Garden.

3

What is an 'Ezer Kenegdo'?

WHEN YOU'VE SUFFERED SPIRITUAL ABUSE, it's very common to have a strong reaction to certain words or phrases, especially those that were used to harm you. For instance, if you were forced to forgive your abuser, the word 'forgiveness' can trigger feelings of great anxiety. Other words like 'honor' and 'submission' can have the same effect if those words were used by others to manipulate and control you. On one hand, we know these concepts are good because they come from God, but we often struggle to accept them because they have been twisted to fit someone else's definition.

For me, the idea of 'help meet' was such a concept. For years, I simply couldn't stand it. I knew the term was scriptural, but I struggled to accept it because the words 'help meet' conjured up images of subjugation and passive surrender. They implied that my husband was more important than me, that his dreams and desires should be elevated above my own, and that his comfort and sexual needs were my number one priority.

The phrase 'help meet' comes from the original English version of the Bible, the Authorized (or King James) Version, which I grew up reading as a child. Eventually, I switched to the New International Version which uses the more palatable phrase, 'suitable helper'. This helped somewhat, but it wasn't until I stumbled across its Hebrew counterpart, *ezer kenegdo*, that I truly began to appreciate the term and the concept. For some reason, I've come to prefer the Hebrew wording over the English, maybe because it's far removed from the dreaded term 'help meet', or maybe because the Hebrew word carries so much richness and depth.

Whatever the case, *ezer kenegdo* is the term I use, and one I hope to introduce to you. Bear with me in this chapter as we dive into some nerdy theology. I promise it will be worth it! One of my favorite pastimes is discussing theology, whether with one of my sisters, a good friend, or a pastor. Nothing invigorates and challenges me more than learning and growing through meaningful discussion, so when I began my research for this book, I chased down two of my friends who were leaders within the Evangelical Free Church of Canada—National Director, Bill Taylor, and National Mission Director, Neil Bassingthwaighte. I knew these men had a storehouse of knowledge and wisdom from which to glean after their many years in pastoral ministry. Sure enough, several Zoom meetings later, my notebook was full of scribbled comments, and much of what I share in this chapter came from our discussions.

So, what is an *ezer kenegdo*?

Let's start with the first word, *ezer*.

UNDERSTANDING 'EZER': A POSITION OF STRENGTH

In Genesis 2, God saw that Adam was alone. The world was teeming with life and animals that Adam has named, but none were found to be 'like unto him.' God looked around and declared:

> "*It is not good that the man should be alone. I will make him a help meet for him.*" (v. 18, KJV)

WHAT IS AN 'EZER KENEGDO'?

So, God decided to create a woman from Adam's rib.

The Hebrew word 'help' is the word *ezer,* a masculine noun which means: 'to rescue or save, to be strong'. Interestingly, the word *ezer* is a derivative of the word *azar,* a verb meaning, 'to help or succour'. While *ezer* (the noun) is found only twenty-one times in the Old Testament, *azar* (the verb) is found over eighty times.

How a word is used helps us understand what the speaker or writer wants to convey. For example, if I used the word 'special' to describe a person, you might initially be confused as to its meaning. But if I used the word repeatedly, or in different contexts, you might soon pick up on the fact that I'm using it as a negative word, and possibly conclude that I'm not a very kind person. In the same way, how *ezer* and *azar* are used in Scripture provides us with valuable clues about God's intention and design for women.

The Verb: Azar

In Scripture, the word *azar* is generally used to describe the action of helping. In many cases, it refers to providing military aid. In Joshua 1:14, for example, Joshua commands all the fighting men to prepare themselves for battle and to 'help' *(azar)* their fellow Israelites conquer the Promised Land. Likewise, when King David was fighting against Saul's son to secure his kingdom, men who once fought for Saul changed allegiance to David. We read that,

> *"They **helped** (azar) David against raiding bands, for all of them were brave warriors, and they were commanders in his army."*
> *1 Chronicles 12:21 (emphasis mine)*

Consider too the account in 2 Chronicles 20:23, where "the Ammonites and Moabites rose up against the men from Mount Seir to destroy and annihilate them. After they finished slaughtering the men from Seir, they **helped** *(azar)* to destroy one another."

Some English translations obscure the word *azar*, making it more difficult to spot. For example, in 2 Chronicles 26:13 we read that King Uzziah had a great army of 307,500 men trained for war, "a powerful force to **support** *(azar)* the king against his enemies." In this scenario, the word *azar* is translated as 'support'.

From these examples in the Scriptures (and there are many more), we get the sense that to 'help'—to *azar*—is to assist with great strength. Warrior-like strength.

The Noun: Ezer

It is interesting then, that God decides to describe Eve as '*ezer*': helper. The same term which is used for warriors and mighty men is used to define a woman.

As mentioned earlier, *ezer* is used twenty-one times in the Old Testament. The first, as we have already noted, is in Genesis 2:18:

> "It is not good that the man should be alone. I will make him a **help** (ezer) meet for him."[15]

A few verses later we read:

> "So the man gave names to all the livestock, the birds in the sky and all the wild animals. But for Adam no suitable **helper** (ezer) was found."
> Genesis 2:20

---

[15] Parentheses and emphasis in this verse and subsequent verses in this chapter are the author's own

That is the last time this word is used to describe Eve, but how it is used the remaining nineteen times in the Old Testament is very interesting. Three times, *ezer* is used to refer to nations, mostly those whom Israel called on for help in wartime. Look at these verses:

> *"Everyone will be put to shame because of a people useless to them, who bring neither **help** (ezer) nor advantage, but only shame and disgrace."*
> *Isaiah 30:5*

> *"When they fall, they will receive a little **help** (ezer), and many who are not sincere will join them."*
> *Daniel 11:34*

> *"I will scatter toward every wind all who are around him, his **helpers** (ezer) and all his troops, and I will unsheathe the sword after them."*
> *Ezekiel 12:14* ESV

Different versions of the Bible translate the word *ezer* in different ways, so you might not realize how frequently the word is used. Generally, however, the English Standard Version consistently translates the Hebrew term as 'helper'.

But perhaps the most interesting and profound use of *ezer* is when it is used to describe God. Out of the twenty-one times *ezer* is used in the Old Testament, sixteen are speaking of God as our *helper*. Let's look at some of them:

> *"I lift up my eyes to the hills, from where does my **help** (ezer) come? My help comes from the Lord, the Maker of heaven and earth."*
> *Psalm 121:1-2*

EZER KENEGDO

"We wait in hope for the LORD; he is our
help (ezer) and our shield."
Psalm 33:20

"Of old you spoke in a vision to your godly one and
said: 'I have granted **help** (ezer) to one who is mighty;
I have exalted one chosen from the people.'"
Psalm 89:19 ESV

"All you Israelites, trust in the LORD – he
is their **help** (ezer) and shield."
Psalm 115:9

"Blessed are those whose **help** (ezer) is the God of
Jacob, whose hope is in the LORD their God."
Psalm 146:5

"You are destroyed, Israel, because you are
against me, against your **helper** (ezer)."
Hosea 13:9

"There is no one like the God of Jeshurun, who rides across the
heavens to **help** (ezer) you and on the clouds on his majesty."
Deuteronomy 33:26

"Blessed are you, Israel! Who is like you, a people saved
by the LORD? He is your shield and **helper** (ezer)
and your glorious sword. Your enemies will cower
before you, and you will tread on their heights."
Deuteronomy 33:29

I invite you to pay careful attention to these verses. Do you see a theme emerging? *Ezer* is always a description of strength.

WHAT IS AN 'EZER KENEGDO'?

When you are in trouble, do you ask for help from someone weaker than you? Do you ask your children to carry heavy boxes for you? Do you ask your elderly neighbor to mow your lawn? Of course not. When we are in need, we turn to people who have the capacity and strength to lend us a hand. Maybe it's our husband or brothers, our father—or in my case, my two six-foot-tall sons. When I struggle to open a jar of pickles, I know exactly who to call; it's someone who has more strength than I.

Throughout the Scriptures, the word *ezer* is used to describe a person of strength, and that applies to Eve as well. Eve was not created to be a weak companion at Adam's side, but to be his strong partner.

One of my struggles came from assuming the term 'help meet' meant being a doormat and a servant. Understanding the true definition of *ezer* helped me to overcome the idea that, as a wife, I was in a position of dishonor. It's hard to be offended at the term 'helper' when God uses the description of Himself. When I think of God as my helper, I don't think of Him as weak or inferior—quite the opposite! And yet, this is the mistake we often make when we think of Eve—and women in general.

At the same time, it is important to understand that nowhere in Scripture does *ezer* mean 'servant'. Just as I would not snap my fingers at God and demand that He serve me (at least I hope I wouldn't), it is not right to read Genesis 2:18 and presume this is how a woman should be treated. Being a *helper* implies someone has a need and someone else has the solution. A helper gives out of a position of generosity and abundance, while the one who receives help is humble and grateful.

In other words, to be an *ezer* carries a sense of honor and dignity. Women as well as men are created in God's image. It's not difficult to imagine God creating Eve and deciding to impart on her an aspect of His divine character. As a parent, I don't get to decide which of my attributes my children inherit. I may wish they inherited my musicality, but I have no power to make that happen. But God did. He designed Eve to carry this aspect of His character because He had a special purpose and plan for her.

Every time Eve helped Adam, she was fulfilling her calling and reflecting her heavenly Father who was, in turn, her *Ezer*. This wasn't a role she could fulfill on her own; she needed the help of the One who created her. So while God is the *Ezer* with the big 'E', she was the *ezer* with the little 'e'. The same is true for us. When we live out this reflection of who God created us to be, we know we are being enabled and assisted by the God who helps us. What a wonderful promise!

What About Men?

Now, you may be wondering, *Aren't men called to be helpers also?*

Yes, they are.

Even though God assigned this specific term to women, it does not mean men are free to take advantage of women or to wiggle out of their own responsibilities. *Ezer* is a masculine noun in the Hebrew language—there is nothing feminine about the word itself. It was used to describe many helpers, including soldiers and warriors. In fact, the Old Testament is filled with stories of men whose names bear the word *ezer* or its derivative.

For instance, the name Abiezer means 'my father is help'. Abiezer was a descendent of Manasseh (Joshua 17:2), but he is also listed in 2 Samuel 23:27 among a group of warriors named 'the Thirty'—men of strength and valor who sided with David when he was running from Saul and hiding in the desert.

Ahiezer is another such name, meaning, 'my brother is help'. His name appears in Numbers 1:12 where Moses calls a man from each tribe to help with a census. Then, in 1 Chronicles 12:3, we see Ahiezer joining David as a 'chief of warriors' in his fight to become king.

WHAT IS AN 'EZER KENEGDO'?

One of the most popular names in the Bible is *Eliezer*, meaning 'God of help'. It appears eleven times in the Old Testament, including in Genesis 15:2 when we are introduced to Abraham's most trusted servant.

These names tell me two things: firstly, that it was common for men to bear the name *ezer*—there was nothing shameful about it. Secondly, these men were likely given their names as a call to fulfill the role of a helper. The meaning of these names tells me that men in early Israel were widely considered to be helpers too—not in any way weak or subservient.

I believe God designed Adam and Eve as equals. Not the same. Not identical, but as equal human beings created to reflect their heavenly Father. In naming Eve an *ezer*, it would seem God is making it clear that she, too, was capable of being a warrior and a help, only, as a woman, her weapons are fashioned out of different materials.

Because women tend to be physically weaker, it's easy to disregard them, but some of the most incredible people I have known are women of deep faith and inner strength. A woman who is a godly *ezer* will fight for her people—her husband, her children, her mother and father, her brothers and sisters, her church, and her community. There is no greater warrior than a woman who falls to her knees and intercedes for those she loves. She is an *ezer*, and she carries the name with dignity and honor because God gave it to her.

UNDERSTANDING 'KENEGDO': A POSITION OF EQUALITY

The second part of the term 'ezer kenegdo' is a bit more difficult to understand. Whereas *ezer* describes who we are (a helper), the word *kenegdo* describes the nature or extent of that help.

Are we a big help? A little help? The King James Version uses the word 'meet', but I find that term difficult to understand. Because of how similar it is in the English language, the term 'help meet' is sometimes referred to as 'help mate', which is an awful translation. *Kenegdo* has nothing to do with being a buddy or a companion.

Kenegdo is difficult to translate because it is not technically a word—it's a phrase. Because this phrase is not used elsewhere in Scripture, we are unable to compare its usage, therefore scholars must do their best with the two verses presented in Genesis. The most common translation is 'similar or corresponding to him'. A further word dive shows that 'corresponding', according to the Collins English Dictionary, means: *to be identical in all essentials or respects, parallel or equivalent.*

'Corresponding' means that, while you are not a man, you are the same as a man in areas that matter. As a woman you have attributes that are unique to your gender, but in the eyes of God, you are of the same value and worth. You are not above a man, nor are you beneath him. You match him value for value, gift for gift, wisdom for wisdom.

Another way to explain this concept is to think of the two wings of an airplane. Which wing is more important? "What a silly question!" you may say. "They are both important. Obviously, you cannot fly an airplane with only one wing." And that is true. Both wings are of equal value, creating balance in the overall structure, and working together to move the airplane in its intended direction. This is a great example of what God intended for the relationship between men and women—both sexes working in tandem, opposite but equal, to fulfill God's commission to be fruitful and increase in number (Genesis 1:28).

Kenegdo, therefore, implies a position of equality. You were created to be a competent helper, able to carry your own load and contribute equally. The contributions you make as a woman are no less important than that of a man.

'EZER KENEGDO': A POSITION OF RESPONSIBILITY

Strung together, the phrase *ezer kenegdo* gives us a clearer picture of the role of women, making it much more difficult to accept the description given in Debi Pearl's book.

We are not inferior or subservient to men; rather, we are created in the image of our heavenly Father who bestowed on us an identity and calling that reflects Him. It is a position of honor. It is a position of strength. And it is a position we must hold with a great sense of responsibility.

You've probably heard the saying, "If mama ain't happy, ain't nobody happy." Perhaps you even have it hanging on a plaque in your house because it makes you chuckle. The problem with this saying is, it's true. As women, we carry tremendous influence in the places we occupy. We carry the power to make or break relationships, build or destroy communities, lift up or tear down the hearts of our children. The impact we have in the lives of those around us is far greater than we often realize.

In later chapters we will explore the damage and fallout that occurs when a woman fails to live as a godly *ezer kenegdo*, but for now, suffice it to say that with great power and strength comes great responsibility. You might be thinking, "But I'm not that important", or "I'm not that strong", or "You must be thinking of other women because I don't have that kind of influence." If that's what you think, I encourage you to keep reading because, dear sister, those words are simply not true.

When I think of a woman, I think of a garden bed—not a flower, like a stately delphinium or fragrant lily—but like the dirt in which they grow. Now before you get too offended, let me explain. When my husband and I bought our acreage a few years ago, it came with a garden filled with all kinds of perennials tucked into the corner by the woods. Years of neglect had left the garden in an awful state. The peonies were limp, the irises refused to bloom, and the delphiniums were thin and scraggly. I had been a gardener long enough to know the problem: my soil was bad.

We soon came to the realization that we had bought twenty acres of hard, dense clay soil, desperately lacking in nutrients. So, we set to work mending the soil. We brought in compost, peat moss, and manure. We trimmed the large pine trees which were blocking the sun, and watered the ground diligently. It didn't take long for the garden to look much different than it had before. What once had been barren and pathetic now overflowed with life, wonder, and beauty.

All because of the soil.

I truly believe women are the soil in the garden of life. When we are healthy and filled with life-giving nutrients, we enable those around us to grow and flourish. But when we are depleted and dry, nothing and no one around us will thrive. This is why it's so important to take care of our spiritual, emotional, and physical health. If we aren't healthy, we will influence those around us negatively. I know this is true because I see what happens in my family when I am having a bad day; I see how the kids hide in their rooms and how my husband slips out to work in the garage—apparently the roar of a tractor is more appealing than a cranky wife.

I have also seen this dynamic play out in church. Many years ago, we attended a lovely church in the countryside filled with beautiful and vibrant families. The longer we attended, however, the more I became aware of an undercurrent of competition and rivalry among some of the women. It was incredibly subtle, and couched in Bible verses, which made it difficult to detect and nearly impossible for a man to notice. Then a new pastor arrived and began the process of getting to know this congregation. He had been there nearly a year when he asked me, "What is going on in this church? I sense something is not right, but I can't put my finger on it." I knew immediately what he was referring to. "The women aren't healthy," I told him, "and they are influencing their husbands."

It grieves me when a church fails to disciple women with the same diligence as it disciples men, or treats women's ministry as an afterthought. Women should be given the same theological training and teaching as men because their health—and the health of their homes, churches and relationships—depends on it! There is a reason why by far the majority of 'influencers' on Instagram are women. It's because that is what we do. We influence. It's our secret power.

So the question is, *Will we use our influence for the glory of God?* We have this tremendous calling and identity, and it comes with honor and great strength, but it also comes with a sober reminder of the responsibility we have to be women of God who love Him, obey Him, and pursue Him with all our hearts.

The more I learn about what it means to be a 'help meet', the more I have embraced this calling and identity. It was given to me by God, and that alone gives me honor. It places me as an equal among men and assigns me the great responsibility of handling this partnership well. I no longer chafe when someone calls me a 'help meet', though I do tend to inwardly translate it and say, "Yes, I am an *ezer kenegdo!*" And you, my friend, are one too.

4

An Identity for All Women

ONE OF THE BIGGEST MYTHS of being a 'help meet' is the idea that it applies only to married women. During my research for this book, I read several Christian authors who touched on the concept of being a 'help meet', and all of them placed it within the context of marriage, as if the description didn't include single women. I, too, believed this myth. Not once, as a young single woman, did I ever think this term applied to me.

I could not have been more wrong.

One of the most exciting discoveries of this study has been the realization that this unique identity is for all women—married, single, divorced, widowed, and so on. How do I know this? Let's take a closer look at Genesis 2 and the order of creation.

THE CREATION TIMELINE

In Genesis 2 we read that God created man first, then gave him responsibility to work in the garden, and then said, "It is not good for man to be alone. I will make a help meet *(ezer kenegdo)* for him" (v. 18, parentheses mine). Then, in verse twenty-two, God created Eve. In chapter three, sin came into the world and Adam and Eve were driven out of the garden. Finally, in chapter four we read that Adam lay with his wife Eve, and she became pregnant (v. 1).

Look at the order carefully.

Before Eve was a mother, *before* Eve was intimate with Adam, *before* she ever drew her first breath, Eve was called an *ezer kenegdo*. God named her *before* He created her.

There was nothing Eve did to earn the position; she merely existed. God's identity for her was placed on her without her having done a single thing to earn it. She didn't have to be a wife or a mother; she simply had to draw breath. Being an *ezer kenegdo* is about being a *woman*, not a *wife*. It's about our gender, not the roles we assume. It's about who God made us to be, and not the circumstances we find ourselves in.

It's also why current cultural conversations about gender are critical. If we believe that gender is fluid, or simply a cultural construct, then we effectively nullify God's design for women. If we cannot adequately define what a woman even is, how will we ever live out our purpose and calling as an *ezer kenegdo*? In later chapters, we will take a closer look at why gender matters, but for now, it's important to realize that your gender—given by God—is connected to your calling and is not interchangeable.

HONORING OUR DIFFERENCES

Just because women are called to be *ezer kenegdos* does not mean we all live it out in identical fashion. *How* we live out this calling will vary according to our circumstances, our culture, and our own giftings and convictions. We are not called to be cookie-cutter Christian women— God is far more creative than that—but we *are* called to live our lives glorifying our heavenly Father in whatever situation we find ourselves.

AN IDENTITY FOR ALL WOMEN

My life in northern Canada will look different to that of a woman who lives in war-torn Ukraine or poverty-stricken Haiti. How I live out my faith and convictions may not look the same as in communist China or in Taliban-governed Afghanistan, or in other places where women do not have the same freedom to confess their faith. We may even have different surface values or convictions, but at our heart, we are *ezer kenegdos* looking to honor God in how we live our lives.

One of my greatest struggles has been the pressure to fit into the mold created by church culture. In my case, being a Christian woman meant: get married, have children, stay at home to care for those children, homeschool the children, tend the garden, do the canning, make your own bread and homemade goods, and sew as needed. Growing up in a Mennonite home, these were the standards we lived by. By themselves, they are good; there is nothing wrong with them. But when these become the standards by which we judge other women, we have stumbled into legalism.

Furthermore, the idea that women should get married, become mothers, and stay at home to care for their children, is grounded in privilege. Not all women have the 'luxury' of staying home. I firmly believe that if a standard is not reachable by all women, then it is not required for holiness. God is more interested in setting standards for our hearts than He is in setting standards for our to-do lists.

Being an *ezer kenegdo*, therefore, is not a one-size-fits-all scenario. How we live out this calling will vary according to our circumstances and season of life.

Women Who Are Married

Since it's widely presumed that only married women are made to be 'help meets', let's take a look at how being an *ezer kenegdo* applies to married women first.

While I have many misgivings about Debi Pearl's book, I did learn something valuable from it. In chapter twelve, she rightly points out that Eve was created to be a 'help meet' *before* the fall, which meant she had the advantage of being sinless and having a perfect husband. Wouldn't that be a dream?! I have often wondered what my marriage would look like if both my husband and I were perfect.

When sin entered the world, however, it didn't dissolve Eve of her calling; it only made it more difficult. Now she had a husband who was sinful and carnal. Now she, herself, was sinful and carnal. But her calling remained the same.

This nugget of truth helped me to understand my role as a wife. In the early years of our marriage, I often reacted to my husband's moods. If he was upset, I became upset. If he gave me the silent treatment, I gave him the silent treatment too. If he stomped around angrily, I bashed a few pots and pans around. If he huffed, I puffed. It was not helpful (or healthy) in any way! But when I read that particular chapter in Debi Pearl's book, I realized I needed to stop. I was not called to mirror my husband's actions or moods; I was called to be a godly woman who stayed devoted to my heavenly Father even when my husband was being a jerk. Being married did not mean our sinful attitudes had to be tied together. Even though we were 'one', I could still make separate choices.

I realized then that pleasing God needed to be my first priority. Understanding this allowed me to unhitch from the unhealthy patterns we had cultivated in our marriage. If we were going to thrive as a married couple, I first needed to live as a disciple of Christ. In fact, I could not be the wife God had called me to be if I didn't put Him first. Pleasing my husband came second, and only if it did not run contrary to God's Word. When we seek to honor Christ first, we are then able to show proper respect and honor towards our husbands, but if we aim to please our husbands first, we will always struggle with feeling like we aren't enough, or that we are failing. As married women it can be a struggle to straddle these two worlds: what my husband needs, and what God commands. When there's conflict between the two, we need to be faithful to obey God's Word.

In the following section of this book, we will study the lives of several women in the Bible who struggled with the challenge of honoring their husbands while obeying God. This struggle may be why the Apostle Paul extolled the virtue of singleness in his letter to the Corinthian church:

> *"I would like you to be free from concern. An unmarried man is concerned about the Lord's affairs—how he can please God. But a married man is concerned about the affairs of this world—how he can please his wife—and his interests are divided. An unmarried woman or virgin is concerned about the Lord's affairs; her aim is to be devoted to the Lord in both body and spirit. But a married woman is concerned about the affairs of this world—how she can please her husband."*
> *1 Corinthians 7:32-34*

If you are a married woman, you have to find a way to live out your calling with a husband who may be wonderful, mediocre, or a jerk. Your calling does not depend on his character; it is between you and God. But *how* you live it out should be evident in all your relationships, and in the case of marriage, your husband should be the primary beneficiary.

The people closest to you should be benefitting from your relationship with Christ the most. If you are married, this means your husband. If

Christ is working in you to produce love, kindness, patience, gentleness, and the remaining fruit of the Spirit, then your husband should be on the receiving end of this outpouring. It may not end with him, but it should begin with him.

But what if he's being a jerk? Insensitive? Abusive?

Being an *ezer kenegdo* means we fight for our husbands. We seek their best. We pray for them. We respect them. We honor them. Sometimes we call the police on them. Insist on counseling. Call them out on their sins. Why? Because we are to fight for their good even when they are unwilling to repent. If we truly love our husbands, we want God's best for them—even if this means they must fail or fall.

But what if you are divorced, widowed or single, and there is no man in your life?

Women Who Are Single

Single women have a difficult time in our Christian culture. Whether it's intended or not, marriage is often elevated as the highest achievement a woman can attain. If you think that's exaggerating, then consider how often a young woman is asked, "Are you dating someone?" Then if she finds someone, it's "How long have you been dating?" "When will you get engaged?" "Have you set a date for the wedding yet?" "When will you get married?"

Is it even possible to be single and attend a family gathering without getting peppered with such questions? By asking, we may think we are showing care, but in reality, we are constantly reminding young women that their value is tied to a ring on their finger. *No ring equals no place in Christian society.*

While we may unintentionally ostracize our single friends, God has not forgotten them. He sees their value and has given them a purpose and calling just like that of married women. Singleness does not feel like a gift when you are struggling with loneliness, but if you are content in your singleness, it can be an adventure in following Christ. Without a husband, how does a single woman fulfill this *ezer kenegdo* calling?

Think back to Paul's words in 1 Corinthians 7. If there's no husband, a woman can devote her energy and creativity to being a 'help meet' in many other ways. Of course, in some ways, she is limited by her responsibilities; she has to think of her own safety, fix her own car, plan her own finances. But in other ways, she is free. She can travel where she wants. She can spend her time as she chooses. She doesn't have to worry about her husband's laundry, or try to not get upset about picking his socks up off the floor. She is free to devote her life to Christ and go where He leads her.

While married women are often consumed with the needs of their husbands, children and households, a single woman has the opportunity to devote herself to God's work with zeal and fervor. This is how she lives her life as an *ezer kenegdo*, serving her church, her friends, her family, and her community. In fact, one of the women we will study in the next section was a single woman who made such an impact on her community that her death not only rocked the church but became the catalyst for a great miracle.

If you are a single woman, believe me when I say, you are an *ezer kenegdo*! Your calling and purpose are wrapped up in your relationship with Christ, and as you pursue His will for you, He will lead you. Your value is not contingent on whether or not you are married. You do not have to earn the right to be a 'help meet', because this is who God made you to be. If you are unsure of what that looks like for you, I urge you to pray and ask God for wisdom; ask Him to show you how and where you can be 'on mission' for Him, because the world is in desperate need of your light and your help.

Believers and Non-Believers

Our identity as an *ezer kenegdo* is established before we are born—therefore, it applies to women who know Christ, and to those who do not know Him or acknowledge Him. You do not have to be a Christian to be an *ezer kenegdo!*

Think of it this way: your children are your children whether they love you or hate you. How they feel about you does not impact their identity. They may reject you, walk away from you, or even despise you, but your DNA flows through their veins. Perhaps it's evident in the colour of their hair, their smile, or the way their eyes crinkle. You may not have a good relationship with them, but that doesn't diminish the ways in which your children fundamentally resemble you.

We know that God loves and desires to be in close relationship with everyone—even those who despise and reject Him. All of us have the privilege of walking with God, talking to Him, resting in Him, calling on Him, relying on Him, crying out to Him. The more we walk with our heavenly Father, the more we reflect Him.

Even those who are not believers have the capacity to reflect their Creator because the fingerprints of God are still on their life, whether they realize it or not. Wherever we see genuine love, care, kindness, patience, goodness and self-control, we see the ways in which all people unwittingly reflect the One who created them. *Any* goodness you see in another human is a reminder that they are created beings who are reflecting their Creator.

You don't have to be a Christian to be a 'help meet', but if you are not, it will be harder to understand the role you are called to fill. You may find it difficult to understand your assignment or be able to accomplish it. Without Christ, a woman will never be able to fully accomplish the calling God has given her because she is not using the greatest resource He offers her—Himself.

A woman who has the Holy Spirit within her and lives in daily surrender and repentance has the advantage of having everything she needs to live a godly life (2 Peter 1:3). Everything we need to be an *ezer kenegdo*, He provides. This enables us to live very differently than women who are not reconciled with Christ. We are not without resources. Those whom God calls, He equips!

ALL WOMEN ARE 'EZER KENEGDOS'

Let me say it again: if you are a woman, you are an *ezer kenegdo*. It doesn't matter if you are divorced, married or single, a virgin, a grandma or a young woman, a believer or an unbeliever, you are a 'help meet'.

In the next section, we are going to look at six women in the Bible who exemplify different kinds of *ezer kenegdos*. Some were godly, righteous women who accomplished great things. Others made poor choices and squandered their calling either through a lack of understanding, or disobedience. As we study their lives, I hope you will begin to see that the identity God gave you is so much richer and broader than you may have imagined. I pray it challenges you to see your life through a different lens and gives you courage to fully live out your calling.

PART TWO

SIX WOMEN FROM THE BIBLE AND HOW THEY WERE A 'HELP MEET'

5

Sarah: It's Complicated

When I thought about *ezer kenegdos* in Scripture and began searching for the perfect example, I realized very quickly that a perfect example was not what we needed. Sometimes, we need an *imperfect* example who we can relate to and learn from. Perfect people can make us feel discouraged, but imperfect people remind us of God's goodness and grace to us despite our failings.

If you grew up attending Sunday School, then the story of Sarah—the wife of Abraham—is probably familiar to you. You may remember her as the old lady who gave birth to a baby when she was far beyond her child-bearing years (although she is not the only woman in the Bible to have that distinction). She was also known for having a temper, and for mistreating her maid, Hagar, after Hagar conceived a son through Sarah's husband, Abraham.

Yes, it's as complicated as it sounds, and it's a good reminder that the Word of God is not just for people who live squeaky-clean lives. In fact, Scripture is a lot like medicine—those who are sick and broken benefit from it the most. Sarah's story is complicated because *she* is complicated. In Sunday School, we tend to present stories from the Bible simplistically which can lead to an over-simplistic view of our favorite heroes. Wisdom may dictate that we withhold harsh realities from our children for a time, but at some point we must help them grapple with the ugly truths and complexities in the lives of our biblical heroes.

Sarah is first introduced to us in Genesis 12 as Sarai, the wife of Abram. Later, after God re-established His covenant with Abram, her name was changed to Sarah, and Abram's name to Abraham. As we continue to read her story, we learn that she was actually Abraham's half sister, that is, she and her husband shared the same father but had different mothers (Genesis 20:12). Sarah was also known for her extraordinary beauty—a fact which is reiterated throughout the narrative because it caused more than its share of problems. But Sarah was more than just the mother of Isaac or the mother of a nation. She was an *ezer kenegdo* who struggled to believe God was who He said He was and would do what He promised He would do.

It is in this same struggle that I find myself relating to Sarah. When God first established His covenant with Abram in Genesis 15, Sarah was seventy-five years old. By this time, her hopes and dreams of having a child of her own had long disintegrated, and in a desperate bid to cling to God's promise, Sarah attempted to manipulate the situation. She approached Abram with her plan:

> "The Lord has kept me from having children. Go, sleep with
> my slave; perhaps I can build a family through her."
> Genesis 16:2

As much as I understand her longing for a child, I struggle to understand this level of desperation. I cannot imagine offering my husband to another woman in an attempt to work out God's plan for my life! *What kind of a woman does this?*

SARAH: IT'S COMPLICATED

A desperate woman.

A woman who has lived with the shame of being barren in a culture that primarily valued women for their ability to have children.

A bitter woman.

A woman who has failed to see the promise of God fulfilled in her life. You can almost taste the bitterness in Sarah's voice when she says to her husband, "The Lord has kept me from having children" (Genesis 16:2). Sarah is blaming God for her suffering. She understood God's sovereignty over all things, including the ability to bear children, and she held Him personally responsible for her misery.

I ask again: *What kind of woman gives up her marriage bed so easily?*

A betrayed woman.

It's difficult to understand Sarah's actions without fully understanding the culture she lived in. But Scripture gives us clues as to how she arrived at her solution. And perhaps this is the point I need to remember: so much of what we do is a reaction to what may seem an insurmountable situation. It's hard to understand someone's decisions unless we hear the whole story.

To understand how Sarah made the decision to give her husband to another woman, we need to backtrack a few chapters in Genesis. When Abraham and Sarah first began their journey to Canaan many years earlier, a famine forced them to take refuge in Egypt. As they were about to enter Egypt, Abraham became worried that his beautiful wife would be taken by the Egyptians, and that he would be killed. He persuaded Sarah to lie on their behalf saying, "When the Egyptians see you, they will say, 'This is his wife.' Then they will kill me but will let you live. Say you are my sister, so that I will be treated well for your sake and my life will be spared because of you" (Genesis 12:12-13).

This is exactly what happened. Thinking she was available and single, Pharoah brought Sarah into his home and took her as his wife. Though the biblical text does not tell us specifically, it appears the marriage was not consummated, but the very fact that a man would offer his wife to another man to spare his own life would cause any woman to feel a bit betrayed. Sarah only escaped this situation when God brought a disease upon Pharaoh's household, causing Pharoah to release her back to Abraham.

You would think Abraham might have learned his lesson after such a narrow escape, but in Genesis 20 we read of a situation where Abraham offered up Sarah *again*. This time, he offered her to Abimelech, king of Gerar, who also took her into his home. In this case, the text makes it clear that the marriage wasn't consummated, and when God intervened, revealing to the king that Sarah was actually a married woman, the king quickly released her back into Abraham's care without harm.

So again, I ask: *What kind of woman betrays her marriage bed and allows her husband to sleep with another woman?*

A woman whose husband has betrayed her to save his own skin, not once but twice! A woman who has learned to do what it takes to survive, even if it means telling a half-truth.

While I may never fully understand Sarah's decision to turn to Hagar as a solution to an unfulfilled promise, I can't condemn her either. Incidentally, when you read the original promise to Abraham in Genesis 15, God doesn't specifically tell Abraham that Sarah would be the one to bear his children. It simply says:

> "Then the word of the Lord came to him: 'This man [a servant of Abraham] will not be your heir, **but a son who is your own flesh and blood** will be your heir.'"
> *Genesis 15:4 (parentheses and emphasis mine)*

SARAH: IT'S COMPLICATED

Perhaps Sarah took this to mean that another woman would be the one to bear Abraham's children, in which case, her solution makes sense, even if it tore her heart apart to suggest it.

The reality is, Abraham should have known better. After all, he personally heard God's promise. But instead of trusting God and encouraging his wife to do the same, he agreed to her proposition. Taking Hagar, Sarah's maid, he slept with her. Once Hagar became pregnant, however, she started to despise her mistress. She understood what it meant to bear Abraham's first-born son and likely imagined a better life for herself as his wife. The text tells us Sarah's reaction, and it shows her distress at the situation. She tells Abraham,

> ***"You are responsible*** *for the wrong I am suffering. I put my slave in your arms, and now that she knows she is pregnant, she despises me. May the Lord judge between you and me."*
> Genesis 16:5 (emphasis mine)

In her distress, Sarah blamed Abraham for her own decision to hand over her maid. Though it was her idea, she did not take responsibility for the outcome. In what appears to be a move to appease his wife, Abraham gave Sarah permission to do as she pleased with Hagar. It is here that we see a more ugly side to Sarah: as one who severely mistreated her maid.

Sarah started out sad and bitter, but at this point in the story. She demonstrates insecurity, jealousy, anger, abusiveness, and a willingness to lie.

And yet, we honor her as the mother of a nation.

How is this so?

It's a good question, and there are a few reasons.

1. Life Is Complicated

Firstly, we need to remember that we are complicated human beings. The way we live, love and grow is often a mixed bag of emotions and decisions. Our path to holiness is not linear, but rather resembles the scribbles of a toddler.

Sarah's journey with God began when she set out with Abraham for the land of Canaan, but by this point in her story, her life is a mixture of faith, fear and failure. While some of her choices leave us scratching our heads, we need to look at how often we, ourselves, struggle to make consistently good choices.

I consider myself to be a fairly pleasant person; I am warm and engaging with most people. But there are times when I have struggled in relationships with others and been cold, distant, and sarcastic. Some people only ever get the sweet side of Maria, but there are others who have experienced my anger and frustration. I am not all things at all times—I am often one thing in this situation, and completely another in another situation.

Sarah may have been a sweet, godly woman, but when it came to Hagar, the claws came out. And instead of the woman of faith we read of in Hebrews chapter eleven, we see a bitter, angry and abusive woman. She was both.

We are complicated humans with a complicated past and with complicated feelings, which is why putting people into a box simply doesn't work. Thankfully, God is more than able to deal with our complex emotions and tend to the wounds in our hearts. Never do we see God berating Sarah for her failings. In fact, we read of God looking out for her, ensuring her safety while in Abimelech or Pharaoh's court, and bringing her back to Abraham. While she struggled to believe and trust in God's promise to her, He remained faithful.

2. God Is Faithful

And this is the crux of it: we may fail and falter, but God remains faithful. When He says He will do it, it will be done!

The older I get, the more I appreciate how vital this truth is. When I was younger, I imagined all the great things I would do for God, but as I have gotten older and seen how badly I have failed my *own* expectations, I realize what a gift God's faithfulness is to His children. If I could screw up my salvation, I would have.

When I reach the throne of heaven, it won't be because I had amazing faith, but because God's hand held me tightly as I squirmed and chafed in my fear. Paul understood this and offers us this assurance:

> *"May God himself, the God of peace, sanctify you through and through. May your whole spirit, soul, and body be kept blameless at the coming of our Lord Jesus Christ. The one who called you is faithful, and he will do it."*
> 1 Thessalonians 5:23-24

Sarah was ninety years old when God's promise to give her a child was fulfilled. What a long and difficult journey had brought her to that moment. Yet as she held her son, Sarah acknowledged the One who made it possible. "God has brought me laughter," she says, "and everyone who hears about this will laugh with me" (Genesis 21:6).

God remained faithful to Sarah throughout those turbulent years. He remained faithful when her faith was immature and lacking. He remained faithful when she failed to act with integrity. He remained faithful when, in her anger and frustration, she sinned against Hagar.

God will be faithful because of who He is.

THE HEART OF A SARAH

I chose to start our character study with Sarah because I figured she would be more relatable to most of us than someone like Mary, the mother of Jesus. I mean, who can relate to a virgin giving birth? Certainly not I!

But I can relate to Sarah—a woman fueled by insecurity and doubt, often caught in the middle of circumstances beyond her control. It wasn't her decision to be handed over to Pharaoh or King Abimelech; in those situations, she was just trying to survive. Sadly, when she did have the power to make her own decisions, she didn't always make the best ones. So yes, I can identify with Sarah. She was a complicated woman who often failed to trust in her heavenly Father.

But before we condemn Sarah for her lack of faith, we need to remember this glorious truth: a little faith goes a long way. Or, as Charles Price says in his book *Christ for Real*, "The most important thing about faith is not the faith, but the object in which we are prepared to place our faith."[16] In the end, a little faith in the right object is a whole lot better than a lot of faith in the wrong object.

Sarah may have failed in significant ways, but she is remembered in Scripture for her faith—not for the *amount* of faith she had, but rather *Who* she placed her faith in. This is the most significant lesson of this study: you and I may be broken women who have made bad choices and now live with the consequences, but when we place our faith, however small, in the person of Jesus Christ, our story can be redeemed.

SARAH: AN 'EZER KENEGDO'

Sarah was not a perfect *ezer kenegdo*. Sometimes she failed, but she is a true example of failing and still winning—not because of her great achievements, but because she placed her trust in God.

---

[16] Charles W. Price, *Christ for Real: How to Grow into God's Likeness,* Kregel Publications, 2011

SARAH: IT'S COMPLICATED

Friend, this is significant . . . and wonderful!

Perhaps you are reading this right now, and you feel like you have failed in your life. Maybe your marriage has failed, and you are now divorced and alone. Maybe you feel you have failed as a mother, and your children no longer speak to you. Maybe you have failed as a friend and caused hurt and pain. Wherever you find yourself today, you can rest in the promise that if you place your faith, even the smallest bit of it, in Jesus Christ, your life still has potential and significance.

God can do so much with a woman who places her faith in Him. He does not hold your past against you. He does not judge you according to your failures. Scripture promises that "if anyone is in Christ, he is a new creation; the old has passed away; behold, the new has come!" (2 Corinthians 5:17, ESV). God is in the business of making all things new, and you are no exception. Whatever hurt you have faced, whatever betrayal has broken you, whatever bitterness you carry, He invites you to bring it to Him. Let Him carry your burdens and allow Him to work in your life and bring you into freedom.

Every *ezer kenegdo* needs to start here. We bring our complicated selves with our complicated problems, and allow our *Ezer*—our Helper—to redeem us. If Sarah's story is your story, then you can be confident that God is more than capable of fulfilling His promise towards you. Will you trust Him?

6

Deborah: A Leader Among Men

If you still think being a 'help meet' is about being sweet and passive, then let me introduce you to one of the most fascinating women in Scripture: a prophetess and judge named Deborah. Her story is unique in that she is the only known female judge to have ruled ancient Israel. She is a perfect example of God using a woman—an *ezer kenegdo*—to be a leader.

In Judges 4, we see Deborah leading Israel at a time when the nation was being oppressed by Jabin, king of Canaan, and his commander, Sisera. Acting on God's instructions, Deborah summons Barak, a commander in Israel, to lead an army of men to fight Sisera and his mighty chariots. Barak resisted at first but eventually agreed and led the Israelites into battle.

The story is interesting for three reasons: firstly, because a woman was leading the nation of Israel; secondly, because an army commander refused to do his job; and thirdly, because in the end, a woman was responsible for Israel's victory. While we don't know much about Deborah, the details we gather from the text allow us to glimpse the way God uses those He chooses. Let's look at what we know about Deborah.

WAS DEBORAH MARRIED?

While some translations of the Bible seem to indicate that Deborah was married, we cannot be sure. In Judges 4:4 she is introduced as "Deborah, a prophet, the *wife* of Lapidoth." The Hebrew word used for wife, *issa*, can also be translated as 'woman' or 'female'. For this reason, some scholars believe the text could just as easily read "Deborah, a prophet, a *woman* of Lapidoth." But there is another complication. The word 'lapidoth' may not refer to a person or even a place. The meaning of this word is 'lamp' or 'fire'. In other words, it is possible that Deborah is being introduced to us as a *woman of fire*. Interestingly, some believe this refers to her original vocation, which may have been preparing the wicks for use in the temple. Or perhaps it refers to her temperament. In either case, she may or may not have been married.

DEBORAH THE PROPHETESS

As a prophetess, Deborah was not alone or unique. Throughout Scripture, we read of other female prophets, such as Miriam (Exodus 15:20), Huldah (2 Kings 22:14), Noadiah (Nehemiah 6:14), Anna (Luke 2:36), and Philip's four daughters (Acts 21:8-9). Female prophets may not have been in the majority, but they were certainly an established part of Israel's society.

The New Testament clearly states that the gift of prophesy is not specific to gender, and goes so far as to ordain women to prophesy. In Acts 2:17 we read,"'In the last days,' God says, 'I will pour out my Spirit on all people. Your sons *and daughters* will prophesy.'" And in 1 Corinthians 11:5 we read, "Every woman who prays *or prophesies* with her head uncovered dishonors her head."[17] The case here seems to be not *if* a woman is permitted to prophesy in public, but that she does so in a respectable manner.

---

[17] Emphasis in these verses is the author's own.

As a prophetess, Deborah would have been intimately acquainted with God. Matthew Henry, in his *Commentary on the Whole Bible*, writes:

> "She was *a prophetess,* that was instructed in divine knowledge by the immediate inspiration of the Spirit of God, and had gifts of wisdom, to which she attained not in an ordinary way: she *heard the words of God,* and probably *saw the visions of the Almighty.*"[18]

We are not told *when* God spoke to Deborah, only that the message He gave her to deliver to Barak was this: "The Lord, the God of Israel, commands you: 'Go, take with you ten thousand men of Naphtali and Zebulun and lead the way to Mount Tabor'" (Judges 4:6). When God spoke to Deborah, she obeyed and relayed the message to Barak. Her obedience was key to being a servant of God.

DEBORAH THE JUDGE

But Deborah was not just a prophet; she was also a judge. As the only recorded female judge in the Old Testament, this places her in a unique position. Matthew Henry suggests that having a woman leading Israel against the nation's enemies may have been beneficial to Israel during this time in their history. Perhaps she was deemed non-threatening, and therefore had more freedom than a man may have been given. Whatever the case, the truth is that God placed Deborah in this specific role and at this particular time for His express purpose.

As a judge, it stands to reason that Deborah was intelligent and educated. She understood the law, she was wise and able to interpret it for the people, she had authority, and she carried out judgement. Obviously, the people of Israel trusted her, and Barak, in particular, depended on her. All through the story, we see a woman of integrity who feared the Lord and obeyed Him.

---

[18] www.christianity.com/bible/commentary/matthew-henry-complete/judges

It is also interesting to note her bravery. Deborah didn't merely send Barak and his men into battle; she participated as well. She volunteered to lure Sisera with his chariots and troops to the Kishon River, where she delivered him into Barak's hands. Since Scripture does not tell us she carried a sword, some believe that is the extent of her involvement, but Scripture does not explicitly say that Barak carried a sword either, yet it is assumed and implied that he did. Whatever her involvement, Deborah was fully immersed in the plan and willing to take risks.

In contrast to Deborah, Barak appears weak and insecure. He refused to go without her, insisting that, "If you go with me, I will go; but if you don't go with me, I won't go" (Judges 4:8). It appears Barak placed more trust in Deborah than he placed in the promises of God. Deborah agreed to accompany Barak anyway, with the understanding that because he refused to go without her, the victory and the honor would be in the hands of a female. In the end, this proved true when Sisera was finally killed by a woman named Jael who drove a tent peg through his head.

It's a thrilling and slightly gruesome story.

What makes this story stand out among the many battles the Israelites fought is the critical role women played in Israel's victory. But even more interesting is the picture of men and women working together to achieve that victory. Barak may have been a commander of the army, but he relied on Deborah for direction and permission. As a prophet, she spoke on God's behalf, giving Barak the strategy for the victory—the *who*, *where*, and *how*. Again, I appreciate Matthew Henry's observation:

> "... (Barak) could do nothing without her head, nor she without his hands; but together made a complete deliverer and effected a complete deliverance."[19]

---

[19] www.christianity.com/bible/commentary/matthew-henry-complete/judges

A COMMON MYTH

It has been said that Deborah held the position of prophet and judge because the men of her tribe were unwilling, lazy, or cowardly . . . or all the above. But a thorough reading of Judges 4 gives no evidence of this. Many would claim that Barak, at the very least, was cowardly in refusing to go into battle without the prophetess at his side. But again, Matthew Henry offers another perspective:

> "Some make this to be the language of a weak faith; he could not take her word unless he had her with him in pawn, as it were, for performance. It seems rather to arise from *a conviction of the necessity of God's presence and continual direction*" *(emphasis mine)*.[20]

The story of Deborah tends to make complementarians twitch a little because it goes against the grain of male headship. Clearly, Deborah was appointed by God—that is undeniable—but it's difficult to explain her position as a leader if your basic premise is that women cannot and should not lead men. So how do we properly understand the issue of women in leadership, and what can Deborah teach us about being an *ezer kenegdo*?

WOMEN IN LEADERSHIP

The story of Deborah usually leads to a discussion about women in leadership, which, in turn, leads to debates among Christians. There are two main beliefs in the church with regard to women in leadership.

1. Complementarianism. In its more extreme form, women are not permitted to have authority over men in *any context*, including within marriage, the church, the family, and the government. A softer form of complementarianism affirms that women are permitted to lead in *certain*

---

[20] Ibid.

contexts and within certain limits. Men are still considered the rightful leaders within the church and home, but women have opportunities to lead (within certain boundaries).

2. Egalitarianism. According to this view, women are permitted to lead in *any capacity,* including within marriage, the family, the church, and the government.

For some Christians, the issue of women in leadership is a secondary issue. For other believers it is an essential doctrine, and any church that allows women to function in leadership roles is practicing heresy. It's not dramatic to say that this issue is divisive and has split churches, but I'm convinced it doesn't need to be this way. In fact, if we view Deborah as just another opportunity to strengthen our debate about women in leadership, we have missed the point entirely. Deborah is not highlighted in Scripture to help us debate whether or not women should be in leadership. I believe Deborah is there to show us that obedience to God may lead us to unexpected places—and sometimes, in contrast to our cultural norms. Deborah shows us that those whom God ordains, He equips, and that God's purposes cannot always be put neatly in a theological box.

DEBORAH: AN 'EZER KENEGDO'

Perhaps the translation is accurate, and Deborah was the wife of a man named Lappidoth. I still think the phrase 'woman of fire' describes her well. She was a woman with true courage and conviction who feared God. Perhaps the biggest takeaway from Deborah's life is the fact that God is not threatened by 'fiery women' and loves to use them to do powerful things for His glory.

Growing up in Mennonite culture and within the evangelical church, I was under the impression that a godly woman needed to be meek and mild, sweet and docile, holy and gentle. This was difficult for a tomboy like me! And, it created in me a sense that I must be broken. I knew for certain I was not sweet or gentle. I wondered for years if there was room in the kingdom of God for a woman who loved to study Scripture, had strong convictions, and wasn't afraid to stand up. *Was I forever doomed to the kitchen or nursery? Was there space within the church for me to serve in my giftings, even if my gifting wasn't in the kitchen? Was I always to remain silent? Was I allowed to teach?* These were the questions I wrestled with for many years.

Deborah is a beautiful example of how creative God is! He could have used a man to help lead Barak to victory, but then we wouldn't likely remember the story. Perhaps God chose to use a woman for the sheer joy of showing His people that He is not limited by our cultural expectations or perceptions of what a woman should be. Perhaps God simply delights in using women who are devoted to Him, whether they are meek and gentle or filled with fire and conviction.

At the end of the day, Deborah reminds us that serving God isn't about pushing the limits of society or whether a woman can or cannot do certain things. She is an example of an *ezer kenegdo* who feared God and lived in obedience to Him, even when it defied the norm. She reminds us that it's not our job to impose limits on anyone—even ourselves! We are called to obey God rather than man. That's how simple it really is.

RELATING TO DEBORAH

You may look at Deborah's life and feel she is completely unrelatable. Maybe she even intimidates you. Or perhaps you are thinking, "Now here is a woman who speaks my language!" and you feel a kinship with her because she displays your kind of fire and courage. She is a reminder that we are all created differently, possess different strengths, and have different personalities, but the one thing we should all have in common is a desire to obey God in whatever assignment or role He gives us.

God may never require you to step into leadership like Deborah did (you may breathe a sigh of relief), but God will ask you to move into areas that are out of your comfort zone. He will work to mold you and sanctify you into a woman who fears Him and obeys Him above all.

This may look different for you than it does for your sister, your friend or your mother, but that's the glory of God's design. No two women are alike. No two *ezer kenegdos* have identical personality or giftings. But we can all be united in our response to God when He calls us, and when we step out into the purpose and calling He has ordained for us, we can be utterly certain He will be with us.

Are you ready to step into obedience?

7

Abigail: A Woman of Integrity

Occasionally you read about a character in the Bible so incredible it's hard to believe they truly existed. Such is the case with the beautiful and intelligent Abigail, the wife of Nabal. I find myself drawn to her story, perhaps because it's not one we talk about very much. It's a story of courage, and highlights the dilemma of a woman who found herself in a difficult situation and married to an awful man.

In 1 Samuel 25, David was on the run and hiding from King Saul. David was not yet king, but his popularity had grown, and to keep a low profile, he and his men had moved into a desert region. There they encountered shepherds who were working for Nabal, a very wealthy but mean and surly man. During their time in the desert, David and his men treated the shepherds kindly and respectfully, ensuring they were protected. Finding themselves in need of supplies and food, David sent a message to Nabal:

> *"Long life to you! Good health to you and your household! And good health to all that is yours!"*
> *1 Samuel 25:6*

David then proceeded to ask for favor, and requested Nabal be generous with his young men and provide for them, since it was a time of festivities. David's request was not uncustomary, but true to his reputation, Nabal responded rudely:

> *"Who is this David? Who is this son of Jesse? Many servants are breaking away from their masters these days. Why should I take my bread and water, and the meat I have slaughtered for my shearers, and give it to men coming from who knows where?"*
> 1 Samuel 25:10

Considering David's popularity, Nabal would have known very well who David was, but in his jealousy and fear, he chose to refuse hospitality. This enraged David, who gathered his men together and prepared to take revenge. One of Nabal's servants, however, ran to Nabal's wife, Abigail, to inform her that David and his men were on their way, and begged her, saying:

> *"Think it over and see what you can do, because disaster is hanging over our master and his whole household. He is such a wicked man that no one can talk to him."*
> 1 Samuel 25:17

Let's stop here for a moment. Clearly, the servants knew their master was an awful man and had likely borne the brunt of his wicked ways in the past. No one knows you better than the people who live with you and who see you in your everyday activities. The servants had most likely seen Nabal's angry and abusive ways before, and this servant knew there was only one person who could help. As Nabal's wife, Abigail was their only hope.

Being the intelligent woman that she was, Abigail understood the gravity of the situation and wasted no time. Quickly, she gathered provisions while telling the servant to run ahead of her. She did not tell her husband what she was planning to do, likely because she knew he would forbid her from doing it. When she found David and his men on the road, she fell to her knees and pleaded for mercy, saying:

> "Please pay no attention, my lord, to that wicked man Nabal. He is just like his name—his name means Fool, and folly goes with him. And as for me, your servant, I did not see the men my lord sent."
> 1 Samuel 25:25

Abigail implored David to reconsider the shedding of innocent blood and sought to appease the situation. Where her husband insulted David, she acknowledged his rightful claim to the throne. Where her husband denied hospitality, she brought gifts of drink and food. Her actions were intended to balance out the damage done by her husband and save the lives of those within her household.

Notice also that Abigail was not in denial about the true nature of her husband—she was completely honest and realistic about his character. She called him wicked and foolish, even though I doubt she did so to his face. She did not sugar-coat his character or attempt to minimize his wickedness. This is so important. David responded,

> "Praise be to the Lord, the God of Israel, who has sent you today to meet me. May you be blessed for your good judgment and for keeping me from bloodshed this day . . . Go home in peace. I have heard your words and granted your request."
> 1 Samuel 25:32-33, 35

Having narrowly averted disaster, Abigail returned to Nabal intending to inform him of what had transpired. She found him holding a banquet, drunk as a skunk, so she told him nothing until morning. When he was sober, Nabal heard the tale of his near demise, and in shock, his heart failed him. 1 Samuel 25:37-38 tells us, ". . . he became like stone. About ten days later, the Lord struck Nabal and he died."

MARRIED TO A FOOL

When I think about Abigail and the situation she found herself in, I wonder how such "an intelligent and beautiful woman", as the Bible describes her, found herself married to a mean, surly, foolish man like Nabal? Likely, in Abigail's case, it was through an arranged marriage. The choice was not hers to make; nonetheless, she was stuck in this arrangement. Stuck in a marriage with a fool.

Perhaps some of you can relate; perhaps you find yourself married to a man who is not wise and makes foolish decisions. The text isn't referring to people who make *a* foolish choice—we've all done that. The text is referring to *a foolish man*.

Proverbs is filled with descriptions of what it means to be a fool:

> *"A fool is hotheaded and yet feels secure."*
> *Proverbs 14v16*

> *"The way of fools seems right to them."*
> *Proverbs 12v15*

> *"Fools mock at making amends for sin."*
> *Proverbs 14v9*

I get the sense that living with her husband's foolishness was routine for Abigail. How many times before had she needed to go behind his back to fix a problem he had created? How many times had she rescued him and covered for him? God had blessed Nabal with a gracious and brilliant wife, even though he did not deserve her. Proverbs 12:4 says that a wife of noble character is her husband's crown, but sadly, Nabal, the fool, was unable to see the gift of the *ezer kenegdo* God had given him.

Having a foolish husband is a difficult situation for any woman, but it is even more difficult if you grew up in a culture where men were placed as the sole authority of the home. What do you do when the leader of your home is a fool? This is a question we must grapple with, and one that I feel we don't discuss enough.

When your husband is wise and loving, it's easy to believe in male leadership within the home, but when your husband is a fool and lives contrary to the Word of God, what then? What is a woman to do? As a church, we must be very careful to give women godly advice in these situations rather than calling them to submit to a man who is sinful and arrogant—not just because men can be foolish, but because they can be abusive, dangerous, even deadly. I do not believe God ever intended for women to submit to abusive and dangerous men, but if we are not careful, that is precisely the message women within the church may be receiving.

ABIGAIL'S DILEMMA

How do we deal with a foolish husband?

In an earlier chapter we discussed how our calling as *ezer kenegdos* does not hinge on marriage or a husband. We are called to be women who obey God, and this becomes challenging when we are dealing with sinful husbands (and also because we are dealing with our own sinful nature).

In our minds, we need to separate what is our responsibility and what is our husband's responsibility. I am not responsible for my husband's sin, but if I cover for him, enable him, or lie on his behalf, I become an accessory to his wrong-doing and therefore become complicit in his sin. His sin, in effect, becomes my sin too.

Abigail may have wrestled with this question long before making the decision she did. We do not know for how many years she struggled to walk with dignity while her husband squandered his reputation. We do not know how many times she discreetly intervened, trying to keep the peace. But we do know that when the moment came, and lives were at stake, she acted in the best interest of those in her care.

WHO DO WE SERVE?

So often as women in complementarian environments, we talk about the idea of being 'united as one flesh' as if we aren't allowed to think separate thoughts or have different ideas from the person we married! But this is not what God had in mind when He created man and woman. God created two distinctly different genders with different mindsets and abilities so we would learn to work together, in unity, for God's glory. But what do we do when, like Abigail, one partner desires to do the right thing and honor God, while the other partner does not care?

First, we must remember that, as 'help meets', we were created by God and belong to God. Because God created us, we are accountable to Him first and foremost. Our calling is no less significant or valued just because we have married a foolish man—though it certainly becomes much more difficult!

Secondly, we have to remember that we serve God first, and our husbands come next. Being a 'help meet' to a godly man who is devoted to Christ is a joy! But when our husbands are foolish, we need to make a choice. *Who will we obey? Whose word matters most? Whose standard of holiness will we follow?*

When it comes down to the wire, we must make the same choice that Peter and the apostles made when they declared before the high priest, "We must obey God rather than men" (Acts 5:29, ESV). I have often heard this phrase used among believers who are taking a stand against government policies they believe are ungodly, but I rarely hear the same Christians use this logic in a troubled marriage.

As an *ezer kenegdo*, we must obey the One who created us. He alone gets the final say in our life. At the end of our days, we will stand alone before our God and give an account for every word and deed. There will be no opportunity to say, "Well, it was my husband's choice." As women, each of us are accountable to God before we are accountable to our husband, and knowing this is the key to living out our calling as an *ezer kenegdo*.

This is the truth Abigail understood, and why she was able to make a critical decision against her husband's wishes. She was called to obey God above her husband, and in doing so, she saved the lives of her family *and* the very man whose foolishness was the root of the problem.

CALLED TO COURAGE

When you are raised in a strongly patriarchal culture where men are elevated as the head of the home, making the choice to disobey takes incredible courage. The natural inclination to allow your husband to lead, even if it's in the wrong direction, is further encouraged by theology which teaches that women are more easily deceived and can't be trusted. If you have been raised this way, you may find it difficult to trust your instincts, because you've been told your whole life that a woman's feelings are untrustworthy.

You may be sensing that your husband is leading you down a path of destruction but feel unable to resist it. You may even wonder if you have the right to do so. But the same Holy Spirit who resides in men and gives them wisdom also resides in women, and a woman whose heart is devoted to Christ can depend on His leading.

Your obedience to Christ matters more than your husband's approval of you. Years down the road, the choices you make now will matter. If you believe your husband is choosing the wrong path, you need to seek wise counsel, perhaps among trusted friends or family, or within your pastoral team, because there may be a point where you need to step back, take a long hard look at the road your husband is choosing, and deliberately choose a different path.

This isn't betrayal. Even if it feels like it. Even if that's what your pastor tells you. Even if those around you are horrified. Sometimes love makes difficult decisions, and sometimes love must be tough and lay down a boundary. We do this, not out of spite, but out of concern for our husband's spiritual health. Is it loving to continue allowing our husbands to sin? Is it loving to allow lies to flourish . . . abuse to grow . . . deceit to take root? Is this love?

The same love that causes us to discipline our children and receive discipline from our heavenly Father, is the love we activate when we confront our husbands in their sin and choose to set boundaries.

It takes tremendous courage to obey God rather than your husband. It takes a strong mind and heart to break away from your spouse in order to do what is right. But I also believe that obedience to Christ is the essence of a true *ezer kenegdo*. Remember, to be a *kenegdo* is to balance our strength with that of a man. When you are pulling together, you can advance together. When he is in sin or fails to do what is right, you use your strength to compensate.

It should be noted at this point that everything we have just discussed can be applied outside of marriage as well. Think back to the airplane analogy. God created men and women to balance each other, and when one side falters, the other must bring back the equilibrium. In a marriage, this happens between husband and wife, but this is also true of relationships within the church and larger community. Women must be willing to call out sin, fight for justice, and speak the truth in the face of foolish men.

This is what you were made for. No doubt if Nabal had known what Abigail was up to, he would have considered it a betrayal, but Abigail's actions were intended for Nabal's good, whether or not he considered them so. Of course, they weren't only for *his* good, but also for those who would have been affected by Nabal's actions. Lives were saved, and Nabal lived to see another day.

WORTH MORE THAN RUBIES

What makes a woman worth "more than rubies"? Is it her obedience? Her meekness? Her complete submission?

Not according to Proverbs 31:10-12. There, it says:

> *"A wife of noble character who can find? She is worth far more than rubies. Her husband has full confidence in her and lacks nothing of value. She brings him good, not harm, all the days of her life."*

It is a wife of noble character.

The word 'noble' comes from the Hebrew word *hayil*, which is used to describe virtue, valor, might, and power. This word describes Abigail well, and it encompasses the heart behind *ezer kenegdo*. We are called to be noble women, and by God's grace, this is who we are, even when our circumstances are less than ideal.

8

Sapphira: A Woman Lost

IN OUR LAST CHAPTER, we looked at an *ezer kenegdo* who defied her husband to save the lives of those around her. In this chapter, we look at a woman who chose to join her husband in deceit and lies, and paid the price with her life.

In the book of Acts we read how the early church was formed and how quickly it grew. Once they were filled with the Holy Spirit, these believers were one in heart and mind (Acts 4:32). A spirit of love and generosity overflowed, and from time to time, those who owned land or a house sold it and donated the money to the apostles so that no one was in need. One couple, Ananias and Sapphira, took note of this and decided to do the same thing. In Acts 5 we read:

> "Now a man name Ananias, together with his wife, Sapphira, also sold a piece of property. With his wife's full knowledge, he kept back part of the money for himself, but brought the rest and put it at the apostles' feet." (v. 1-2)

Notice a few things. Firstly, it appears that the decision to sell the property was a joint decision between Ananias and Sapphira. Ananias did not make the decision without his wife's knowledge, though he certainly could have done so without her permission. Secondly, the text clearly states that Sapphira was fully aware of her husband's decision to keep back part of the money. It appears they even rehearsed their version of the events to corroborate each other's story.

But the apostle Peter, through the power of the Holy Spirit, discerned the truth and confronted Ananias saying:

> *"How is it that Satan has so filled your heart that you have lied to the Holy Spirit and have kept for yourself some of the money you received for the land?" (v.3)*

Notice Peter wasn't angry because Ananias chose to keep back a portion of the sale; he was angry that Ananias deceitfully presented his portion as the full amount: "You have not lied just to human beings but to God" (v.4). When Ananias heard this, he fell down and died, and a few young men within the congregation wrapped up his body, carried him out, and buried him (v.5-6).

For whatever reason, no move was made to inform Sapphira that her husband had died. Perhaps God had revealed to Peter the truth of the situation, or maybe he was giving her an opportunity to prove her innocence. Whatever the case, about three hours later, Sapphira appeared before Peter with no knowledge of what had just happened. Peter questioned her, "Tell me, is this the price you and Ananias got for the land?" (v.8).

Sapphira didn't know it at the time, but this was the most critical moment of her life. This was her opportunity to tell the truth. But as we sometimes find out in life, those moments are fleeting and often we do not recognize the significance of them until it's too late.

"Yes," she said, "that is the price" (v.8).

Peter said to her, "How could you conspire to test the Spirit of the Lord?" (v.9). And at that moment, she fell down and died, and the same young men who had buried her husband only three hours prior, buried her as well. Acts 5:11 says that "great fear seized the whole church and all who heard about these events."

I can't help but think that is an appropriate response, because this isn't just a story about a foolish man and a foolish woman; it's a reminder that we can't fool God. We may be able to fool those around us into thinking we have it all together, that our children are perfect, that our marriage is wonderful and our finances are secure, but God knows the truth. He sees all, and nothing can be hidden from Him.

But let's backtrack to an element in the story that pertains to being a 'help meet'. The most important fact is not that Ananias sinned—we have already talked about foolish husbands, and clearly, Ananias was foolish. This story is different because now we have an example of a wife who was also foolish. A woman who followed her husband in his sin and paid the same price.

This story hits hard because of how closely it hits home.

At some point in my childhood, my mother found out about the abuse that had happened to me and did nothing about it. Sometimes I think her betrayal was worse than the abuse itself, because I expected her, as a woman, to understand and intervene.

I have seen this pattern repeat itself throughout Mennonite culture. Men who are abusive or alcoholics are often supported by women who either look the other way or participate in their husband's sin. This isn't a matter of being unaware or in the dark about your husband's choices; it's about having full knowledge and doing nothing. It's about being complicit, either by your silence or by your active participation.

There is no foundation in Scripture to support a woman taking refuge under her husband's wing when it comes to accountability. Many years ago, I had a conversation with a woman who alluded to the fact that, because her husband was the 'head of the home', she wasn't responsible for what happened within it. She reasoned that it was her job to be submissive, and assumed that when she stood before God, she would be able to use this reasoning to excuse herself.

But Sapphira's story is evidence that being a married woman is not a 'get out of jail' card. While Ananias was the one who sold the land and brought the money to the apostles' feet, he did so with the *full knowledge* of his wife. She knew. Not only did she know; it appears they rehearsed their answer beforehand so that when she stood before Peter, she already knew what she was going to say. Deceit was in her heart long before it left her lips. Sapphira had already determined her direction with the full expectation that she would get away with it.

But God sees all.

He sees the difference between a woman trapped in a foolish marriage who longs to do what is right, and a woman married to a foolish man who follows him in his folly.

WHEN WOMEN ARE 'BAD'

While cooking supper one day, I asked my teenage boys if they could name five evil men in history. They easily named Adolf Hitler, Joseph Stalin, Pol Pot, Heinrich Himmler, and Jack the Ripper. Then I asked if they could name five evil women, and they couldn't. I couldn't either, can you?

Why not?

Perhaps it's because we live in a world ruled by men, so women are less likely to come to a place of such power that they are able to inflict pain and suffering on a large scale. Perhaps it's because we tend to view women as warm and nurturing, and dismiss the few stories of abuse we have heard. Perhaps it's because we believe women are victims in a male-dominated world, and can't easily believe a woman could be evil.

Since Romans 3:10 says, "There is no one righteous, not even one," it shouldn't surprise us that women go astray, and yet it often does. I would add that while there may be no fundamental difference between what lies in a man's heart and a woman's heart, how a woman tends to behave is often vastly different due to her physical abilities. If she can't use her physical strength, a woman bent on destruction can use other weapons at her disposal such as gossip, manipulation, and lies.

History has certainly seen its share of evil women. Think of Queen Mary I (or, 'Bloody Mary'), best known for her relentless persecution of Protestants and burning over three hundred religious dissenters at the stake. Or consider the Countess Elizabeth Bathory, known as the 'Blood Countess' because of her incredibly cruel torture of peasant girls. It is believed she killed upwards of six hundred and fifty girls through shocking means and was never brought to justice because of her family's wealth and connections. Or what of Ilse Koch, a German war criminal? She was infamous for her horrific treatment of prisoners at Buchenwald prison during World War II, earning her the nickname, 'The Witch of Buchenwald'.

In more recent years, we have Griselda Blanco, drug lord of the Medellin Cartel, who was implicated in the death of over two hundred rivals. Or women such as Rosemary West, Aileen Wuornos, Genene Jones—all serial killers—who targeted children, women, and men. Even today, we struggle to understand women who are involved in the human trafficking of young girls for the purpose of sex—women such as Ghislaine Maxwell, who was found guilty of partnering with Jeffrey Epstein to traffic underage girls.

Women like Ghislaine are vital to abusers because they are seen as less dangerous, someone who can be trusted and therefore can more easily persuade a young girl or potential victim to co-operate. Research suggests that up to one third of human traffickers are women, with the number rising in Eastern Europe and Asia to sixty percent![21]

Some women who participate in sex trafficking were victims at one time, but not all women who are involved in this industry have been trafficked themselves. Some women are *supporters* (silent but non-interfering) while other women are *partners* (actively participating in criminal activities). In many cases, particularly in Asia and Africa, women are the *madams*—the sole operators and managers of their trade. Within this abusive system there are women who are enablers, abusers, and victims.[22]

There is something profoundly disturbing about a woman who kills and destroys. Perhaps it's because God placed within her the capacity to give life, and to see her destroy it creates a paradox between the call to nurture and the desire to kill.

THE POWER OF A WOMAN

Because we live in a world where women are often victimized and at the mercy of men (this is particularly true in some cultures more than others), it's easy to forget that women have the same potential to be evil. It can be tempting to paint all women as weak victims while forgetting the tremendous power and influence they carry.

This is especially true when we consider the nurturing power of a mother or a woman who is a primary caregiver. Several months ago

---

[21] Jeglic, E. L., Ph.D., Understanding the Role of Women in Sex Trafficking, Psychology Today, December 30, 2021

[22] Ibid.

while having coffee with a friend, I asked her, "Who do you think does more damage: a narcissistic mother or a narcissistic father?" I knew her relationship with her mother was as complicated as my relationship with my father. I wanted to know which parent—father or mother—she thought inflicted the worst damage on a child through their abusive ways. Without hesitation, she replied, "mothers."

This led to a fascinating conversation and the discovery of Adam Young, a licensed social worker who currently works with the Allender Center and hosts *The Place We Find Ourselves* podcast. On his blog, Adam discusses what he calls 'The Big Six'—six different needs children look to their parents to meet and that are necessary for healthy emotional growth.

These six basic needs are:

1. Attunement—knowing what your child needs.

2. Responsiveness—attending to your child's needs.

3. Engagement—pursuing your child's heart.

4. Ability to regulate—soothing (or stimulating) a child in distress.

5. Strong enough to handle negative emotions—welcoming a child's spoken and unspoken emotions.

6. Willingness to repair—owning and rectifying failures and seeking to repair when there is a rift.

He writes that, "... as a child, your most important attachment was your connection with your primary caregiver. This one relationship shaped your brain more than anything else."[23]

---

[23] Young, A., "Attachment: What It Is And Why It Matters", www.adamyoungcounseling.com/attachment-what-it-is/

Because women tend to be the primary caregivers of children (obviously, there are exceptions), we are given the incredible privilege and responsibility of guiding and teaching them. Our response to our children has the ability to impact them for life! We can do great harm to our children if we, ourselves, are unhealthy and toxic. An unhealthy mother is unable to provide for her children because she cannot even take care of herself. She will pass her destructive habits on to her children who will pass them on to their children until someone dares to stop the cycle.

Even if you do not have children of your own, you will understand this to be true when you consider your own relationship with your mother. What impact has she left on your life? How did she empower you? How did she hurt you? What did you learn about love, marriage, life, finances and relationships through her? Was she critical? Abusive? Emotionally negligent? Or was she caring, attentive, and loving?

If you experienced a secure childhood with loving parents, you may struggle to understand how a parent could be abusive, especially a mother. But if you have experienced abuse by one or both of your parents, then you understand the life-long damage that abuse leaves behind.

At first I wasn't certain my friend was correct. Can a mother really do more damage than a father? But when I considered those in my life who experienced abusive fathers versus abusive mothers, I decided she may be onto something. Obviously, both are incredibly damaging, and I do not want to minimize anyone's experience with an abusive father, but I believe that a mother does have the power to minimize the damage inflicted by an abusive father if she puts the needs of her child first.

Abuse by a father is made worse when it is enabled by a mother. Maybe it's because we expect more of our mothers. We rely on them for our primary needs as a child, and when we experience neglect or abuse, it cuts like no other betrayal. If you have experienced this wounding as a child, then you personally know the extent of damage a woman can do.

LIVING OUT OUR CALLING

We need to remember that women can, and have, and will continue, to do evil and cause pain, because they are sinners also. While we have learned that *all* women are *ezer kenegdos,* we need to be realistic about the fact that not all women are *godly ezer kenegdos.* Many women have disobedient and rebellious hearts. They have no desire to walk with God or live by His commands. They are *ezer kenegdos* who are not living in accordance with their identity and calling, and the damage they inflict can be great and merciless.

Remember that you and I are under no obligation to live as women of God. God does not coerce His creation into obeying and surrendering to Him. He gives us the freedom to choose whom we will serve and obey. The choice is ours, and so are the consequences.

While it is a mistake to view all women as unstable or sultry 'Jezebels', it is also a mistake to put them on a pedestal of modesty and virtue. Women are much more complex than that! We are sinners. We are saints. We can be gentle. We can be cruel. We can be a safe place to land, or the hand that bites you. Perhaps the paradox is that we can be a mixture of all these things. We may be bitter, selfish, manipulative, coy, pouty, jealous, and demanding. We may justify our behavior because of the hurts of our past. We may play the victim when we are, in fact, the perpetrator. Maybe we are the victim *and* the perpetrator! Again, we are complex beings, but in the end, God knows our hearts and judges accordingly.

As an *ezer kenegdo,* Sapphira failed to remember that her first loyalty was to God. Obedience to Him should have trumped obedience to her husband. Her duty was not to obey her husband regardless of what he did or didn't do, but to obey God and live surrendered to Him. God, in His grace, offered her an opportunity to choose a different path. She had a moment, however brief, to make things right.

It reminds me of the words in Deuteronomy 30:19-20: "Now choose life, so that you and your children may live and that you may love the Lord your God, listen to his voice, and hold fast to him."

But she didn't.

Sapphira's story is a sobering reminder of our responsibility as *ezer kenegdos*. She reminds us that there is a time and a place to oppose those who are in authority. She reminds us that we are the other wing of a plane, designed to bring balance and order when the first wing fails. We cannot be 'yes' women to the men in our lives; we must be women who consistently point others to Christ, remind them of what is good and true, call them to repentance when they sin, and above all, refuse to join them in their folly!

9

Priscilla: A Woman of Faith

IF THE LAST CHAPTER DEPRESSED you as it did me, then I hope this chapter encourages you and reminds you of the amazing legacy a woman of God can leave.

One of the things we often forget is the incredible number of women who are mentioned in the New Testament as being co-workers in Christ. While some argue that Paul is a misogynist (strongly biased against women) for ordering women to be silent in church, I believe Paul was actually progressive for his time.

The Jewish culture was highly patriarchal, but through the laws He gave to Moses, God was enabling dignity and protection for Jewish women. The Roman culture, however, did not truly value woman. In their culture, women were property to be owned and had no rights within their marriage, family, or community. In the early days of the church, the Gospel was particularly appealing to women, widows, and slaves because of its message of equality and freedom. Paul was instrumental in spreading this message. In fact, his declaration, "There is neither Jew nor Gentile, neither slave nor free, nor is there male and female, for you are all one in Christ Jesus" (Galatians 3:28) was as radical as could be at that time!

When you study Paul's life, you see that he included women in his ministry. Everywhere you look in the New Testament, you find Paul acknowledging the presence and contributions of women in the early church. And none more so than his friend Priscilla.

Priscilla, one of the most frequently mentioned women in the early church, is introduced to us in Acts 18. After spending some time in Athens, Paul traveled to Corinth where he met a Jewish man named Aquila. Aquila, along with his wife, Priscilla, had recently moved to Corinth after Emperor Claudius ordered the Jews to leave Rome. Paul went to visit this couple and we read that, "because he was a tentmaker as they were, he stayed and worked with them" (v.3). This implies Priscilla and her husband were both involved in their tentmaking work.

After some time, Paul left Corinth along with Priscilla and Aquila, and arrived in Ephesus, where the married couple stayed while Paul sailed on. While living in Ephesus, Priscilla and her husband visited the synagogue, where they heard a young man, Apollos, preach. They realized that, while he had a thorough knowledge of Scripture and taught about Jesus, he only knew about the baptism of John. So the couple invited him to their home and "explained to him the way of God more adequately" (Acts 18:26). Aquila and Priscilla established a home church in Ephesus, which we read about in 1 Corinthians 16:19. Later, in his letter to the Romans, Paul singled out this couple:

> *"Greet Priscilla and Aquila, my co-workers in Christ Jesus. They risked their lives for me. Not only I but all the churches of the Gentiles are grateful to them. Greet also the church that meets at their house."*
> *Romans 16:3-5*

There are several significant observations we can make in these short verses, that illustrate Paul's respect for Priscilla and her dedication to the Gospel.

AN EQUAL PARTNER

Firstly, we note that Aquila is never mentioned alone. In the text of Scripture, he is always connected to his wife, Priscilla. Sometimes Paul refers to them as "Aquila and Priscilla" and sometimes as "Priscilla and Aquila"—but they're always together. This implies an extraordinary level of teamwork and partnership in a culture where husbands were considered the head of the home.

Secondly, Priscilla and Aquila demonstrate God's original intention for marriage. "This is why a man leaves his father and mother and is united to his wife" (Genesis 2:24). Being 'united' implies a spirit of oneness within the marriage, with both partners pulling in the same direction. Of course, we know this isn't reality for many marriages, but it *was* God's original design. Nothing creates more conflict in a marriage than two individuals acting like . . . well, two individuals, each dedicated to their own desires and following their own paths.

What we see in the life of Aquila and Priscilla is a pulling together for the sake of the Gospel. United in heart and ministry—what a beautiful picture of a godly marriage!

At the time of writing, my local church is searching for a new pastor, and as someone who sits on the committee, it's been an interesting process. One of the main questions we ask a candidate's referees is: *Is his wife supportive of his ministry?* We ask this because we know how crucial it is for a pastor to have a wife who embraces his calling. It doesn't mean, however, that she needs to play the piano or serve on a variety of committees. A church must not presume that by hiring one pastor they get two workers, but it is important that a wife supports her husband. Ministry work is hard; the help of an *ezer kenegdo* lightens an already heavy load.

Priscilla, however, was not a pastor's wife. In fact, some scholars maintain that by naming Priscilla first, Paul indicates that she played a greater role in their home church than her husband. In Paul's day it was virtually unheard of for learned men to acknowledge women in their writings at all, but to write a woman's name before her husband's was even more unusual. It implies that Priscilla was not just a disciple but a leader among the early church.

A TEACHER OF THE GOSPEL

We get the sense that Priscilla was not only instrumental in leading the church within her home, but also in teaching Apollos. Look back at Acts 18:26:

> "When Priscilla and Aquila heard him, **they** invited him to **their** home and explained to him the way of God more adequately." (emphasis mine)

Not only do we see Priscilla mentioned first, but the use of the plural 'they' shows it was not only Aquila who invited and explained but also Priscilla. For the lack of a better phrase, she was 'in there like a dirty shirt', taking part in what many consider to be males-only territory.

Some might argue it was okay for Priscilla to teach Apollos because it was within her home, not behind a pulpit, but I don't believe that argument holds up. What did a New Testament church look like? It was mostly based in homes, without pulpits, a worship team, or all the things we consider to be essential to our worship services today. Women were instrumental in hosting churches, and Paul gives greetings to other women who hosted churches in their homes, including Lydia, the founding member of the church in Philippi (Acts 16). In these settings, it's not impossible to believe that women had a huge role to play in spreading the Gospel, and it wasn't just by serving tea. They were disciples just as much as men, and they played a vital role in the early church.

Paul clearly believed women were full partners in the Gospel, as is evidenced by the many women he enlisted in his ministry. Women were influential and were given leading roles within the early church. One of the most interesting examples of this is the entire chapter of Romans sixteen, where Paul greets his many co-workers in Christ. Of the twenty-nine people listed in this chapter, ten of them are women, and as Marg Mowczko points out,

> "Seven of the ten women are described in terms of their ministry (Phoebe, Prisca Priscilla, Mary, Junia, Tryphena, Tryphosa, Persis). By comparison, only three men are described in terms of their ministry (Aquila, Andronicus, Urbanus), and two of these men are ministering alongside a female partner (Aquila and Prisca, Andronicus with Junia)."[24]

She goes on to say,

> "It is apparent that women were active in significant ministries in the church at Rome. It is also apparent that Paul has no problem with these women. Rather, he affirms them and their ministries."[25]

It is also interesting to note that not a single woman is mentioned because of her status as a mother or married woman. Paul lists these women because of their partnership in ministry, which gives even more

---

[24] Marg Mowczko, www.margmowczko.com/list-of-people-in-romans-16_1-16/, May 18, 2019

[25] Ibid.

evidence that our marital status really isn't the most important thing about our life.

WHAT IT MEANS FOR US TODAY

The extent to which a woman is permitted to lead within a church depends on how we read and understand Scripture. Most conservative churches tend to hold to a complementarian view—the idea that women can be active within the church but only under male leadership. Other denominations have a more generous view of what a woman is permitted to do, and the debate between these two positions is often fierce and heated.

I prefer not to choose either side in the debate because I think in doing so, we miss the big picture: God has invited all His disciples to the table and given all of us a mandate through the Great Commission.

> "Then Jesus came to them [the eleven disciples] and said, 'All authority in heaven and on earth has been given to me. Therefore go and make disciples of all nations, baptizing them in the name of the Father and of the Son and of the Holy Spirit, and teaching them to obey everything I have commanded you. And surely I am with you always, to the very end of the age.'"
> Matthew 28:18-20 (parentheses mine)

Even though the Great Commission was originally spoken to eleven disciples, most teachers and pastors understand it to be a mandate for *all* believers. The Great Commission does not only land on the shoulders of men; it is also for every woman who has surrendered her life to Christ. In her blog post titled, *Women: The Great Commission is Your Permission,* Bible teacher Lisa Bevere writes:

> "The Great Commission *is* permission; it doesn't require a building or an organization, and this mandate is inclusive of

both genders. In Christ all are called and liberated to declare God's good news."[26]

This calling to make disciples is for you, whether you are complementarian or egalitarian. For the complementarian, the calling is outworked within the boundaries of male leadership. For the egalitarian, there are no such limits. Either way, what matters is that you find a way to live out the Great Commission in your life, because the world—and the church—needs you to operate in your giftings.

I believe women are essential to the fulfillment of the Great Commission. For too long we have been taught that our greatest contribution is raising children for the next generation. The life of Priscilla shows that there is plenty of scope for us to contribute in other ways. In a blog article, *Why Pastors Need Women Teachers (And Vice Versa)*, Jen Wilkin highlights why women are essential to the health and growth of the church. Directing her thoughts to a room full of male pastors, she gives these four reasons:

> *1. She is an example you cannot be.* When a woman sees someone who looks like her and sounds like her, teaching the Bible with passion and intelligence, she begins to recognize that she, too, can love God with her mind . . . Women who only hear men handle the Bible well sometimes forget to consider themselves capable of doing the same.
>
> *2. She brings a perspective you cannot bring.* When men teach, they naturally draw on examples that resonate with men . . . but a woman teacher might also speak the language of Jane Austen movies and HGTV. And she'll probably draw a few different observations from the text than a man might.

---

[26] Lisa Bevere, "Women, The Great Commission Is Your Permission", www.lisabevere.com/blog/women-the-great-commission-is-your-permission/

3. She holds an authority you cannot hold. A woman can tell other women to stop making idols of their careers or families in a way you can't. A woman can address other women on vanity, pride, submission and contentment in a way you can't . . . She can say things like "PMS is not an excuse for homicide" and not get a single nasty email the following day.

4. She sees needs you do not see. In the week-to-week arena of her ministry, a woman teacher will gain a feel for the pulse of the women in your church . . . A woman teacher can give you insight at the ground level.[27]

CALLED TO USE OUR GIFTS

A wise pastor will have gifted women in leadership roles and encourage the women in his church to use their spiritual and natural gifts because they are given to build up the church. Some of the women I know in leadership are gifted in managing finances, teaching, and are trained counselors. Their contribution to their church is invaluable.

There are so many ways in which a woman contributes to the life-giving mission of the church. In conservative circles, we tend to focus on hospitality, raising a family, and discipling other women. In more egalitarian circles, women are often free to teach and preach. But the main point is that we all live out the Great Commission to the extent that we understand it, and to remember once again that our obedience is to Christ and Him alone. He has given us gifts to use for the building up of the body, and I suspect His boundaries for how a woman can use her gifts is far more generous than some believe it to be.

---

[27] Wilkin, J., "Pastors Need Women Teachers (And Vice Versa)", www.thegospelcoalition.org/article/pastors-need-women-teachers-and-vice-versa, October 17, 2013

I am not interested in controversies or arguments, but I am interested in pursuing the Great Commission as I believe God has directed me to do. At the end of the day, I am not going to stand before men to give an account of my life, but I will stand before God.

How about you? What gifts has God given you to share within the church? How are you living out the Great Commission in your corner of the world?

Priscilla is a beautiful reminder that a woman devoted to Christ and using her gifts is essential to disciple-making. As an *ezer kenegdo,* she devoted herself to Christ and served the church in her house, along with her husband. How thankful I am for her example!

10

Dorcas: A Beloved Woman

CAN YOU BE SINGLE AND still be an *ezer kenegdo?* I firmly believe the answer is yes! I believe Genesis 2:18 is an invitation for every woman to understand her foremost identity, and it has nothing to do with marriage or motherhood. Unfortunately, within evangelical culture (and most definitely within Mennonite culture), single people often feel isolated or devalued because of their marital status.

Why is this?

In an article discussing the perceived curse of singleness, Pastor Greg Morse points out that, according to Deuteronomy 28:15-18, barrenness was considered a curse from God. He writes:

> "Singleness was seen as a dead end. To be single was to functionally blot out one's own name from under heaven because you wouldn't continue your lineage through your children."[28]

God's command in Genesis 1:28 to be fruitful and multiply could only be fulfilled in the context of marriage. After all, you can't be fruitful and

---

[28] Greg Morse, "Singleness was a Curse", www.desiringgod.org/articles/singleness-was-a-curse, August 27, 2018

multiply all by yourself. For this reason, singleness was seen as a very undesirable situation. But when Jesus came, He flipped the narrative. In the eyes of His fellow Jews, He was a failure. Not only did Jesus die a criminal, He died without leaving an heir. But through the redemptive work of the cross, Jesus demolished every barrier, whether between male or female, Jew or Greek, free or slave, married or single. All now stood on equal ground before Him.

In Christ, we have become a spiritual family. This shifts the focus to growing and nurturing spiritual children. We are still called, according to the Great Commission, to be fruitful and multiply, but this is no longer limited to biological children—it is a mandate to increase our spiritual family and grow the kingdom of God. The early church understood this and organized their lives around this new way of thinking. Not only did they challenge social hierarchies, they also elevated those who may have been considered 'less than'—including women.

In Acts 9, we meet a presumably single woman who impacted the lives of many and lived out her calling as a 'help meet' despite not being married. There's not a lot written about Dorcas, but what we glean from Scriptures is enough to teach us several important truths:

> "In Joppa there was a disciple named Tabitha (in Greek her name is Dorcas); she was always doing good and helping the poor. About that time she became sick and died, and her body was washed and placed in an upstairs room. Lydda was near Joppa; so when the disciples heard that Peter was in Lydda, they sent two men to him and urged him, 'Please come at once!'
>
> Peter went with them, and when he arrived, he was taken upstairs to the room. All the widows stood around him, crying and showing him the robes and other clothing that Dorcas had made while she was still with them."
> Acts 9:36-39

Peter sent the crowd away, got down on his knees and prayed, then he turned to the dead woman and said, "Tabitha, get up" (v. 40). And she arose.

It's so easy to get caught up in this remarkable miracle that we forget the woman to whom it happened. *Who was she? Why did she matter?*

Joppa was a seaport city, with people of many different nationalities and languages. Having both a Greek and Hebrew name would not have been unusual in that setting. Interestingly, both *Dorcas* and *Tabitha* mean 'gazelle'. Even more notable is how Dorcas is initially introduced, as if her being a disciple was the most important fact about her. Not only was Dorcas a disciple, it appears she was a prominent and well-loved disciple known for her kindness and service to others. Her death created such a wave of grief that when the disciples in Joppa heard that Peter was nearby, they sent two men to urge him to come and help.

There is a high likelihood that Dorcas was single, probably a widow. In Roman society, single women had limited ways to produce their own income; the fact that Dorcas made clothing for the poor suggests she was a woman of some means. Widows were often left a sizable inheritance after their husband's death. This would have given her the financial freedom to care for those who were less fortunate.

THE CHURCH'S VIEW ON SINGLENESS

According to the United States Census Bureau, nearly fifty percent of adults in the United States are single. That number comes to around 126.9 million men and women who are single, either by choice or circumstance.[29] This number is a sharp rise from previous decades. One of the reasons for this is that women are becoming more highly educated

---

[29] "Unmarried and Single Americans Week: Sept 17-23, 2023", Press Release Number CB23-SFS.135, https://www.census.gov/newsroom/stories/unmarried-single-americans-week.html, September 17, 2023

and they no longer live in a society where marriage is economically necessary. They want to marry for love, not convenience.

With this many single people in our midst, we must consider how the church is reaching them. Statistics show that, in general, church attendance in North America is declining, and for the first time, it tends to be women who are leaving the church.[30] This includes single women.

This is in sharp contrast to the history of the church where Christianity was seen as a refuge for women in a male-dominated culture. Within the family of God, women were treated with dignity and allowed to participate in significant ways. So I have to ask, what has changed? If the early church was able to provide a place of community and belonging for single people such as Dorcas, then how is it that we no longer do so?

In her book, *The Making of Biblical Womanhood*, Dr. Beth Allison Barr traces the history of women within the church. A professor in medieval history at Baylor University, Dr. Barr challenges the perception that the church has always taught women to stay home and raise children. As a historian, Barr contends this is simply not true.

As the early church grew and began tying itself to political structures, the role of women in the church was reduced, and largely given to men. While women were limited in how they could serve, there was an exception made for unmarried women—virgins—who were considered pure and untainted by sexual contact. Some of these women became nuns or abbesses who devoted themselves to preaching the Gospel and serving the church.

Dr. Barr asserts that during that time a hierarchy of women developed, with virgins (single women) seen as more godly, followed by widows and lastly, married women and mothers. Virgins were seen as women

---

[30] Mcclendon, D. "Gender Gap in Religious Service Attendance Has Narrowed in U.S." Pew Research Center, May 13, 2016.

who were devoted to Christ and were therefore given more freedom to preach the Gospel. Widows were vital to the ministry and had a great deal of influence because of their generous financial contributions to the church. Wives and mothers were seen as less valuable because of their inability to contribute and because their days were consumed with family duties.[31]

But all this changed during the Reformation.

Dr. Barr explains:

> "Women have always been wives and mothers, but it wasn't until the Protestant Reformation that being a wife and a mother became the 'ideological touchstone of holiness' for women. Before the Reformation, women could gain spiritual authority by rejecting their sexuality. Virginity empowered them. Women became nuns and took religious vows, and some, like Catherine of Siena and Hildegard of Bingen, found their voices rang with the authority of men. Indeed, the further removed medieval women were from the married state, the closer they were to God. After the Reformation, the opposite became true for Protestant women. The more closely they identified with being wives and mothers, the godlier they became."[32]

The Reformation brought winds of change, not only for the church but for the family structure. Where once it was considered necessary for the priest to stand between the members of his congregation and God, the people now understood Jesus Christ to be their high priest. As this change swept the church, it affected the status of women. Martin Luther firmly believed a wife should stay at home, saying:

---

[31] Dr. Beth Allison Barr, "The Making of Biblical Womanhood", Theology in the Raw Podcast Ep.968

[32] Barr, B. A., Dr., *The Making of Biblical Womanhood: How the Subjugation of Women Became Gospel Truth*, Brazos Press, 2021

"Just as a snail carries its house with it, so the wife should stay home and look after the affairs of the household."[33]

By elevating the role of marriage, Luther elevated the roles of wives and mothers but not necessarily the role of women themselves. Where once the priest stood between a wife and God, now her husband was considered her advocate. While men had their position strengthened (because they had direct access to God), in many ways, the women were left in the same or in a worse situation.

All these changes affected the long-standing hierarchy between women. Now married women (especially those with children) were considered of most importance, followed by widows, and at the bottom of the ladder were single women with no husband to advocate for them.[34]

Has anything changed since then?

I'm not so sure.

A quick scroll through Instagram, a casual glance at the attendance on Sunday morning, or a peek at a typical women's conference, and you will see the focus towards married women or mothers. Our current church culture is not kind to single women. Instead of being a welcoming space, we have driven single women to the back-row seats and into the lonely corners of church community.

Whether we intend it or not, church culture has heightened the status of marriage and motherhood, much to the pain and detriment of single and childless women. We inflict damage when we say things like, "A woman's highest calling is motherhood" or "You'll never find anything as satisfying as motherhood." We are essentially telling a single or

---

[33] Susan C. Karant-Nunn and Merry E. Wiesner-Hanks, *Luther on Women: A Sourcebook*, Cambridge University Press, 2003

[34] Dr. Beth Allison Barr, "The Making of Biblical Womanhood", Theology in the Raw Podcast, Ep.968

childless woman that, without children, her life will amount to nothing. If we believe marriage and motherhood is 'our highest calling', we make it difficult for these women to fully participate in the body of Christ.

When you consider the women we have studied so far—Deborah, Abigail, Sapphira and Priscilla, the Bible is strangely quiet about their status as mothers. The same is true for Dorcas. *It's as if being or not being a mother is not the most important fact about them.* Perhaps it's because being a mother is only a small aspect of womanhood, not the entire sum of it. Perhaps there is more to women than the status of their womb and the ring on their finger. Perhaps we have misjudged what it means to be single *and* a 'help meet'.

A BIBLICAL VIEW OF SINGLENESS

Within the church, singleness is often viewed as a deficiency, or a stage of life you hurry through as quickly as possible. This is particularly ironic when you consider that we have all been single at some stage in our life, and at least half of us will be single again in the event our spouse passes away before us.

When God created Adam, He saw that it was not good for Adam to be alone. He was surrounded by creatures of all kinds, but there was no one 'like unto himself' (Genesis 2:18).

Author Dani Treweek says it best:

> "The reason God knew that it was 'not good for man to be alone' was because he had created Adam with the exact need to not be alone. Think about that for a moment: An all-powerful, all-knowing God could have chosen to create this human creature to be entirely self-sufficient, to have no need of anything or anyone else. But he didn't. Instead, he created Adam to need others who were like him. So, God created another human person made in

the divine image, magnificently like the man but also wonderfully distinct from him in meaningful ways. God created woman."[35]

When God created woman, it was for the purpose of being a 'help meet' or *ezer kenegdo*—not just for the purpose of being a companion or a lover.[36] And yet, when we think of being a 'help meet', our minds often go in that direction.

Dani Treweek goes on to say,

> "The first human being didn't simply need a spouse. He needed other people. Adam alone couldn't achieve what God had created him to do. So, the answer to his aloneness was not the meager provision of a single marriage relationship but the holistic resolution found in a multiplicity of interpersonal human relationships."[37]

Treweek is arguing that Adam's needs went beyond the need for companionship. He needed community. He had a mission in life, and he was not equipped to do it alone. He needed a helper who would assist him.

This need for fellowship is what made Dorcas such a vital part of her Christian community. She wasn't created to merely be a companion or to fulfill the sexual needs of a man; she was created to be a helper who would contribute to her community and, in return, receive the love and companionship she also needed. This highlights how God's plan for the church goes beyond marriage and how it encompasses people from all walks of life.

---

[35] Treweek, D., *Adam's Aloneness Wasn't Just His Singlehood*, Christianity Today, July 8, 2022

[36] Ash, C., *A Biblical View of Marriage*, The Gospel Coalition, July 8, 2022

[37] Treweek, ibid.

When Paul writes, "There is neither Jew nor Gentile, neither slave nor free, nor is there male and female" (Galatians 3:28), you get the sense that our position in society matters very little to God. He is far more concerned with our position in light of the cross. When human distinctions are used to devalue people, we must work to dismantle those systems and show that, at the cross, the ground is level and accessible to all.

In God's kingdom, women are not valued according to the number of children they have. A single woman possesses every promise in Christ that a married woman has, and can live in the same freedom and grace as any mother. In fact, Paul remarks that, though it is good to be married, "I wish that all of you were as I am" (1 Corinthians 7:7). He believed it was better to be single and devoted to the Gospel than to be married, for he knew the challenges that often come with marriage.

THE GIFT OF SINGLENESS

Once we get past the mentality that being a 'help meet' means being a wife and mother, then we can ask ourselves: *What does an 'ezer kenegdo' look like as a single woman? Who can I help? Who can I serve?*

My friend Linda is a beautiful example of a single woman who has embraced her calling as an *ezer kenegdo*. She has used her gifts to serve the church through singing, teaching Sunday School and serving on the board as a trustee, and has become an indispensable part of our church family. During a family crisis, she opened her home to her three nieces and devoted the next few years to raising them. To say she is an *ezer kenegdo* is an understatement.

When I think of Dorcas, I think of Linda. I think of their devotion to their family—physical or spiritual. I think of the impact their sacrifice has made, whether they are aware of it or not. I think of how they are fulfilling their identity and calling as 'help meets'.

When Paul made the comment that he wished all were single just as he was, he was likely referring to the fact that "the harvest is plentiful but the laborers are few" (Matthew 9:37). We live in a lost and broken world, and as wives and mothers we often get sidetracked thinking about what we will make for dinner, helping a child with a science project, taking another child to the dentist, or all the other family distractions—to the point where we lose sight of the big picture, the fact that *people need Jesus*. Who has time to tell their neighbors about Jesus when the house needs to be cleaned and there are cookies needed for the school bake sale?

Paul understood that singleness can be a gift. It allows the sort of focus and devotion which married couples cannot give. To be single is to be a laser. Whereas a lightbulb lights up a whole room, a laser concentrates all its energy into one beam of light, making it possible to cut through steel. A single woman, unencumbered by the responsibilities of marriage and parenting, can choose to direct her energy and focus on a single issue, and like a laser, be incredibly powerful and effective.

No doubt, singleness comes with its daily challenges—who to sit with in church, where to spend the holidays, who's going to help you fix the car . . . But it comes with deeper challenges as well, and this is where the body of Christ should be operating in community and opening our arms to embrace the entire family of God. Dorcas poured out her life to serve those around her, and in her hour of need, the community in which she had invested her life fought to save her.

If you are a single woman reading this, may I encourage you to step into the calling and identity for which you were created? A quick history lesson will show you that some of the most formidable women in missions have been single women. Think of Lottie Moon, Amy Carmichael, Mary Slessor, and Gladys Aylward. Their devotion to the Gospel and to Christ gave them the courage to blaze trails in foreign countries and endure exceptional hardships.

But you don't need to be called to the mission field to make a difference. It is possible to be an *ezer kenegdo* in whatever circumstance you find yourself in. Ask yourself:

Who has God placed in front of me that I need to love?

What ministry is He calling me to serve in?

What mission field is God placing on my heart?

Then may I encourage you to boldly step into this calling and embrace the identity for which you were created!

PART THREE

LIVING YOUR CALLING AND LEAVING A LEGACY

11

Our Identity Matters

THE IDEA OF IDENTITY IS a hot topic in our current culture. Wherever you hear the discussion, whether on social media, in movies or books, or even in politics, one thing has become very apparent: there is an identity crisis in our culture. While we may get tired of hearing about identity, understanding it *is* important. It impacts our lives and determines how we will spend our time and energy in the future. Understanding our identity is key to living our lives as God intended.

We are all born with an identity but are often unaware of it until we become a little older. Babies have no concept of who they are, and toddlers believe what they are told. As we grow and mature, we start to become aware of our family, our friends and our culture, and how we relate to them. This growth happens rapidly during the teenage years—a vital time in our lives, as we explore different ideas and question who we are.

In the Merriam-Webster dictionary, identity is defined as: 'the distinguishing character or personality of an individual'.

What distinguishes you? What makes you who you are? What differences are there between you and someone else?

While humans have many similarities, we each have qualities that help define us. Some of these qualities may be *biological:* tall or short, red or black hair, and so on. Or they may be connected to our *beliefs:* Mormon, Mennonite, Muslim—even atheist, or any other religion. They could include aspects of our *personality:* shy, introvert or extrovert, kind, thoughtful, or any other traits. Or they could include our *gifts and strengths*: musical, athletic, academic, creative, and so on. Each of these represents an area of our life, helping us form a picture of who we are.

Having a healthy sense of identity is key to living a healthy life. If we don't know *who we are,* then we will fail to understand what our purpose on earth is. But before we dive into that, let's take a look at the different voices which may influence our sense of identity.

WHO THE WORLD SAYS I AM

Who does the world say you are? I promise that if you don't know, the world will happily tell you!

The problem with allowing those around us to define our identity is that they don't really know the inner us. They only can judge based on what we present and what they see. Based on appearances, they are likely to hand out labels to identify us. Some of these labels may be true, but some labels may be false.

What happens when we present a false version of ourselves?

In the world of social media, it's easy to pretend. In fact, there's good money to be made if you can present a version of yourself that appeals to the masses. Millions of dollars can be made if you have the ability to transform yourself into a brand and market yourself to the right target group. The result is often an online version of ourselves versus the person we are in real life, in our homes.

OUR IDENTITY MATTERS

The pressure to present ourselves as one thing online can make it easy to forget that we are not who the world says we are. The world only cares about who we are as long as it benefits in some way; this is why our identity must never be rooted in what our culture tells us. Not only does contemporary culture not understand *who* we really are; it tends to tell us what we want to hear.

Another pitfall of a false presentation of yourself is the loneliness that comes when the world (and your friends) buy into the filtered version of you that you are selling. If you want to be truly known, then you must present yourself with authenticity.

I am reminded of a conversation I had with one of my sisters as we discussed our tendency to present a tough exterior in the middle of difficult circumstances. To our friends and those in our church we came across as competent and confident, but at home we dissolved into tears. We finally came to the realization that it wasn't the church's fault for not understanding our pain; we had sold a false version of ourselves which those around us bought.

Not only does the world not see you, it also tends to label you in ways that aren't helpful. Our culture seems incapable of having complex and nuanced conversations; it seems easier to label someone rather than take the time to get to know them intimately. Rather than ask why you are against abortion, you are labeled 'anti-choice'. Rather than seek to understand why you believe in justice, you are labelled as 'woke'. Rather than dive into the complexities of Scripture in a discussion on women in leadership, you are labeled either 'progressive' or 'conservative'.

The world would rather label you than seek to understand you, and in the process, impress upon you an identity you didn't ask for. In the eyes of the world, I am a victim. 'Too much' for some, and 'not enough' for others. Too liberal for some, and not conservative enough to others. Too bossy, too timid, too loud, too quiet. If you allow these voices to dominate your mind, you will never find out who you are because you will have spent all your time trying to be who everyone else thinks you should be!

Our culture has constant suggestions about who we *should* be. Through the world of advertising and social media we are encouraged to be thinner, more beautiful, more educated, more powerful, an influencer, a boss babe, a hot mama, or many other suggestions.

When people throw such labels at us, we have a choice as to whether or not we want to accept those labels for ourselves. Sometimes it feels like Satan is throwing a wet noodle against a wall just to see if his ideas will stick. We have the authority and the right to refuse the labels that Satan, the world, and even our well-intentioned friends throw at us. It won't stick until we allow it to stick.

If we want to truly know who we are, we are going to have to quiet the voices of those around us. To make it even more challenging, not only do we have to quiet the voices around us, we also have to contend with the voice inside of us.

WHO I SAY I AM

If I were to ask, "Who are you?" how would you answer?

If I had to answer the question I would fumble a bit, because I'm more comfortable answering the question, "What do you do?" than answering questions about my identity. I would probably give an answer like, "I'm Jim's wife. I'm a mother. I am a musician. I am a Mennonite. I am a daughter, a sister, an aunt . . . even a great aunt. I am a teacher, a writer, a pianist, a gardener, a decent cook."

But these aren't my identity. These are the roles I have assumed in life. They are not the same thing.

OUR IDENTITY MATTERS

Pastor Mark DeJesus observes that:

"Often we confuse our identity with a role we have in life. We invest so heavily in this role and mistake it for our identity."[38]

It is only when we face a crisis that we tend to review these roles and realize how much of our self-worth and identity we have attached to a role such as being a wife or a mother. It is far easier to think in terms of roles than it is to think deeply about our identity.

The topic of identity becomes particularly important when we consider the rise of gender dysphoria in our culture. In much of today's discourse, the idea that you can change your gender is widely accepted. You may biologically be a woman, but if you feel like a man or identify as a man, then you have the freedom to choose that, or vice versa.

According to a study published in the *American Journal of Public Health*, one out of two hundred and fifty adults in America, particularly young adults, feel their gender identity does not match the sex assigned them at birth.[39] Another study estimates that 1.3 million adults over the age of eighteen and 1.4 million youth between the ages of thirteen and seventeen identify as transgender.[40] This staggering number indicates just how many people are redefining their gender identity. Additionally, it is becoming more and more difficult for our culture to articulate and define what a woman is.

As the line between who we are biologically and what we feel becomes increasingly blurred, figuring out our identity is even more of a challenge.

---

[38] Mark DeJesus, "8 Signs You Are in an Identity Crisis", www.youtube.com/watch?v=PEGaXcmmZew, 20 Oct, 2020

[39] Esther L. Meerwijk and Jae M. Sevelius, "Transgender Population Size in the United States" etc., American Journal of Public Health 107, 2017

[40] Herman, J. L., Flores, A. R., & O'Neill, K. K. "How Many Adults and Youth Identify as Transgender in the United States?" www.williamsinstitute.law.ucla.edu/publications/trans-adults-united-states/, June 2022

It would seem that even we, ourselves, are not a reliable or consistent voice in establishing our own identity. One of the results of not knowing who we truly are, is an increase in depression and anxiety. You can be sure, however, that God carefully designed you and wove together every aspect of your being, including your gender.

WHO GOD SAYS I AM

Before sin entered the world, Adam and Eve had a clear understanding of who God was and who they were. But sin muddied the waters of understanding, and they could no longer see their reflection. Having lost sight of who God was, mankind began to wrestle with their own identity. Because we are created in the image of God, it is essential that we know who God is! The more we know who He is, the more we understand who we are. Once we lose sight of God, we lose sight of who we were meant to be.

The only one who truly has the authority to label us is God. He is our Creator and our Father, and as such, He alone has the understanding and authority to name us. Imagine you are a potter and you are molding a lump of clay. You know exactly what you want to make—you have been dreaming of a beautiful vase to give to your mother as a gift. So you set to work with your hands, carefully, lovingly crafting an exquisite work of art.

But once you are finished, your beautiful vase decides it would rather not be a vase. Your vase looks around the room, notices all the other beautiful vases, and decides it is not necessary. Instead, it wants to be a pot for cooking soup. *Who gets to decide what it was created for? The creator . . . or the created?* It's quite ridiculous to think of a creature choosing for itself when the creator knows the ultimate plan.

And yet, we are often guilty of doing the same thing to God. We reject the identity with which He made us, either because we don't understand it or because we are driven by our selfish nature to pursue an alternative. In rejecting our identity, we reject our purpose.

Understanding who we are in Christ begins with accepting the Bible as God's Word to us. When we read Scripture, we find there is so much more to us than we first thought. The truth is far more precious than anything we could conjure up ourselves.

Who does Scripture say we are? Neil Anderson provides a helpful list in his book, *Living Free in Christ*.

> "According to Scripture, you are ... a child of God (John 1:12), a friend of Christ (John 15:15), a saint (Ephesians 1:1), complete (Colossians 2:10), free from condemnation (Romans 8:1-2), a citizen of heaven (Philippians 3:20), born of God and untouchable by the evil one (1 John 5:18), salt and light on the earth (Matthew 5:13-14), a branch of the true vine (John 15:1), chosen and appointed to bear fruit (John 15:16), God's temple (1 Corinthians 3:16), God's coworker (2 Corinthians 6:1), seated with Christ in the heavenly realm (Ephesians 2:6) and God's workmanship (Ephesians 2:10)."[41]

This is who God says you are, and His Word should outweigh the voices of your inner self and of the world around you. Whenever there is a discrepancy between the identities we claim and God's Word, we must allow God's Word to trump our thoughts.

One thing we must remember is that, because our identity is so precious, Satan will do anything to discredit or destroy it. We see his strategy in Matthew 4 where Jesus is in the wilderness for forty days and nights. Knowing Jesus had just endured a long stretch of time without food and that His body was physically depleted, Satan came after Jesus. Attempting

---

[41] Anderson, Neil T., *Living Free in Christ*, Gospel Light Publications, 1993

to tempt Him, Satan began by casting doubt on Jesus' own identity: "If you are the Son of God, tell these stones to become bread" (v. 3).

When that didn't work, Satan tried again. This time, Satan took Jesus to the highest point of the temple and said, "If you are the Son of God, throw yourself down . . ." (v. 6). Notice how Satan begins by questioning Jesus' identity as the Son of God.

If you are . . . If you are . . . if . . . if . . . if.

But then it appears Satan tries a new strategy. Unable to cast doubt on Jesus' identity, he now bargains for what he knows Jesus wants. He shows Jesus the kingdoms of the world and their splendor. "All this I will give you," he says, "if you will bow down and worship me" (v. 9).

We need to be aware of Satan's strategy: first, he will attack our identity, and when that fails, he will try to find another weakness within us. If we remain confident in who God says we are, he will fail in his attempt to distract us from our purpose and calling.

However, it's important to remember that there is a difference between being given an identity, and accepting it.

ACCEPTING OUR IDENTITY

When my daughter was younger, one of our favorite movies was *The Princess Diaries*, a classic tale of a young girl unaware of her true identity. Our heroine is living a simple life with her mother and navigating all the complexities of being a teen, completely unaware of her status as a princess, when her grandmother, the Queen, arrives, turning her life upside down and causing her to question everything she thought she knew.

I wonder if this is true of us. How many Christians live unaware that they are, in fact, royalty? How many women spend their days not realizing they are daughters of a King? How many young girls have never known the identity to which God has called them? They grow up accepting the labels placed on them by others, but fail to understand who they really are.

Just because we do not know or accept our identity as an *ezer kenegdo* doesn't mean we aren't one—it simply means we are missing out on our calling. Our calling and identity are inexplicably linked. If we don't understand *who* we are, we will never understand *what we are called to do*. You cannot live out your calling if your identity is in question.

Do you remember the old television series, *Mission Impossible?* Every episode would start with the main character receiving a message which said, "Good morning Mr. Phelps. Your mission, should you decide to accept it, is to . . ." and then they would be off on some ridiculously difficult mission.

In some ways, this is my challenge to you. God wants you to accept the identity He created for you, and He has a mission, a purpose, and a calling for you to fulfill. But it's your choice whether you want to accept it or not. It's probably going to be ridiculously hard. It's going to require more than you can give. It's going to take resources and abilities beyond what you have, but it's also going to be the beginning of a journey with Jesus which will have significant and eternal implications.

Are you ready to hear about your assignment?

12

Our Calling Matters

UNDERSTANDING YOUR IDENTITY IS the first step to finding your calling. You will never know what you are called to unless you have made peace with God and surrendered your life to Him. Once you have aligned your life, heart and will to His purposes, God will lead and guide you.

Young people, especially teens who have grown up in the church, are often consumed with a desire to know, "What is God's will for my life?" or "What is my calling?" I'm fairly certain these questions are also asked by adults who have not yet found their purpose or are unsure of what God has called them to do.

Before we can discern *what* we are called to do, we must first answer the question of *who* is calling us.

WHO IS CALLING?

I really hate answering the phone. Mostly, because it's only telemarketers who call these days. My friends know me well enough to text, but only the dentist and scammers call my home phone. I know when I pick up the phone that someone is calling me. The call isn't coming from out of the blue; it originated at a certain location from a specific person.

When we talk about our calling in Christian circles, we need to acknowledge where the call originates from. Who is calling us? The answer may seem obvious to you, but I think at times it's possible to misinterpret God's voice, just like Samuel did.

In 1 Samuel, we read about Samuel the prophet, who, as a little boy, heard a voice in the night. He did not understand where the voice came from and wrongly attributed it to his mentor, Eli the high priest. After several attempts and with help from Eli, Samuel came to realize the voice calling to him in the middle of the night was God's.

Samuel didn't know or understand where the call came from, but once he was aware, he responded to it. In the same way, we need to be aware of who is calling us or we won't be able to respond appropriately. In 1 Peter 2:9, we read:

> *"You are a chosen people, a royal priesthood, a holy nation, God's special possession, that you may declare the praises of him who called you out of darkness into his wonderful light."*

And in 2 Thessalonians 2:13-14, Paul writes:

> *"We ought always to thank God for you, brothers and sisters loved by the Lord, because God chose you as firstfruits to be saved through the sanctifying work of the Spirit and through belief in the truth. He called you to this through our gospel that you might share in the glory of our Lord Jesus Christ."*

These verses make it clear that it is God who calls us. He chose us. He saved us. And now He invites us to participate in a kingdom mission.

How do I know when God is calling me? Often, it's when an idea comes to me, and it won't leave me alone. Even as I pray about it, the feeling grows stronger and heavier. If it's just my idea or a random thought, the heaviness goes away within the hour or a few days, but when God calls me to a task, it stays with me even though I try to distance myself from it. There is a persistent lack of peace until I agree with God and obey what He has asked me to do.

CALLED TO *BE*

When God calls us, it's not just to accomplish His heavenly to-do list. His plan for us isn't simply that we do more work or strive to accomplish more. Rather, He calls us first to be His children. Sometimes, in the rush of my day to day, I forget that I am not a human doing but a human being, designed to live with the Spirit of God flowing through me, creating in me a new spirit and a new heart.

As His child, I am called to be holy (1 Corinthians 1:2), to be free (Galatians 5:13), to live in peace (1 Corinthians 7:15), and to have eternal life (1 Timothy 6:12). God is more concerned with my heart than He is with my to-do list, and as someone who struggles with insecurity, that is wonderful news. When I focus on being God's child, I am less distracted by the weight of my daily responsibilities and more intent on being the woman God wants me to be—allowing the Holy Spirit to move me to be a person of joy, peace, love, patience, kindness, and all the other fruits which are unattainable when forced. Life seems simple when I strip away the excess and focus on simply *being* God's child.

So when I get confused as to what my calling is, I try to remember that first and foremost, I am called to be His child. If I forget this truth, everything gets a little cloudy. But when I am secure as His child, I find an excess of love in my heart that naturally spills over and positively effects those around me. Works alone will not save me, and if I focus only on works, I will soon find myself exhausted and discouraged. In contrast, when I anchor myself in Christ and enjoy my relationship with my heavenly Father, those same actions flow effortlessly from me. They are the fruit of my faith, but not the source of it.

It is one of life's ironies: if you focus on doing good works, you will grow weary and faint. If you focus on abiding in Christ, you will be energized to do good works. True faith always finds a way to express the work of the Holy Spirit within us, and while God is more concerned about our hearts, He also calls us to action.

CALLED TO *DO*

According to Ephesians 2:10, God has a specific plan and purpose for you and me and has given us gifts and talents to share with the world. When we think of the work we are called to do, we often forget it will be something that not only glorifies God but brings joy and contentment to our hearts because we know we are fulfilling our purpose. It might not always feel like work because it comes so naturally to us, and yet what is natural to you may be completely foreign to someone else. For years, I lived with the unspoken fear that my life purpose would be something I despised, as if being miserable was a virtue. At some point, I began to recognize the true nature of God; He is loving, gracious, merciful, and He delights in His children. And I believe He delights in seeing His children use their gifts.

It is wise to remember, however, that our calling is going to require some measure of sacrifice. It won't always be easy. The Apostle Paul had an extraordinary ministry, but he also suffered greatly for the sake of his calling. He was beaten, imprisoned, stoned and shipwrecked, among other hardships. Most of us will never suffer like Paul, but we should be prepared to be challenged when we step into the mission to which God has called us. At times our faith will be tested, and we will be tempted to abandon our calling and replace it for one that costs or demands less.

But if we turn off course, we will not finish the race God has set for us, and we will miss out on hearing Him say, "Well done."

Paul could endure his suffering because he recognized his calling came from God. Any calling that originates within us will die quickly in the face of opposition, but when God places a call on your life, you can trust He will enable you to complete it.

CALLED TO BE AN 'EZER KENEGDO'

So far, we have been talking generally about believers, but what does this mean for us as women? Now that we have a clearer picture of the identity God gave women, how do we apply this calling to our lives? What does it look like in practical terms?

Before Jesus ascended to heaven, He gave his remaining eleven disciples what is known as the Great Commission. We find it in Matthew 28:18-20 where Jesus said,

> "... all authority in heaven and earth has been given to me. Therefore, go and make disciples of all nations, baptizing them in the name of the Father and of the Son and of the Holy Spirit, and teaching them to obey everything I have commanded you. And surely, I am with you always, to the very end of the age."

It's interesting to note that only eleven male disciples were given this command (v. 16), and yet the church throughout the ages has understood it to be for every believer. The clue is in the phrase, "to the very end of the age." This commission remains, generation after generation. It is the mission of every believer, missionary, and church.

Including women.

What Jesus didn't say was, "Men, go and make disciples while the women make dinner." In fact, Jesus made a point of being inclusive towards women, accepting them in ways which were unusual in His culture. One of my favorite examples is found in Luke 10 where Jesus is invited to the home of two sisters, Martha and Mary. While Martha busied herself in the kitchen, Mary sat at Jesus' feet, listening to what He said. When Martha complained, "Lord, don't you care that my sister has left me to do the work by myself? Tell her to help me!" Jesus replied by saying, "Martha, Martha . . . you are worried and upset about many things, but few things are needed—or indeed only one. Mary has chosen what is better, and it will not be taken away from her" (v. 40-42).

There are a few things to consider here. Having people sit at your feet while you taught was common for a rabbi and his students, so the fact that Mary was sitting at Jesus' feet implies that she was acting like a student—unheard of among Jewish teachers for women of that time. Secondly, when Martha came to interrupt, Jesus not only affirmed Mary's choice, but made it clear it was the better choice!

I think about this every time a man insinuates a woman's place is in the kitchen, because according to Jesus, it is not. I am first and foremost invited to be a disciple at His feet.

In every recorded interaction with women, Jesus was kind and gracious. He loved them all, without extending shame or condemnation. In fact, apart from His mild rebuke of Martha, I cannot find a single instance where He uttered a harsh word towards a woman. Any harsh words Jesus uttered were reserved for the religious, hypocritical leaders—who happened to be men. Jesus' treatment of Mary as she sat at His feet, and His decision to be revealed in His resurrected body first to a woman, shows that He considered women valuable. They were welcomed among His disciples and followers, and the Great Commission was handed to women in equal portion to men.

One of the main reasons for writing this book is that I believe women have largely misunderstood their role in the Great Commission. We have often positioned ourselves simply as bystanders while the men do the heavy lifting. Because of our cultural biases, we have tended to think that staying at home, making supper and taking care of children is the *only* way to fulfill God's calling on our life. I believe we have allowed ourselves to be put in a box which is much too small and constrictive. Remember, the Great Commission is *your* permission!

WHAT IS YOUR CALLING?

You are called to be a child of God.

You are called to be His disciple.

You are called to do this as an *ezer kenegdo.*

If you are still struggling to understand your purpose, consider the following questions: *What do you do that brings you joy? How can you share that joy with others?* Sometimes, that's all it takes—a small gesture shared with others. Maybe no one will notice, but I assure you, any step taken in love and obedience will produce fruit. The work God has called us to is not meant to be a burden but a privilege, and when it feels like a burden, it is often because we have forgotten an important truth: we cannot do it alone. God has not called you only to abandon you. Rather, He invites you to come just as you are and place all that you have in His hands so that He can carry the burden while you rest in His strength.

Will you surrender it all to Him?

13

Our Legacy Matters

If I told you that you don't have to have what it takes to fulfill your calling, would that discourage you? Let me assure you, it's actually a good thing!

It's better to come to the Lord empty-handed and say, "Use me, Lord, however you want" than to come with arrogance and pride. God can do wonders with an open heart that is fully devoted to Him. He doesn't need you to be highly educated or charismatic, or to have a large bank account. He is not looking for over-achievers, or women who have their act together. He simply needs *you*, able and ready. In fact, I would argue that people who are naturally gifted leaders, competent, strong, intelligent and efficient, have a much more difficult time allowing God to use them because it's more difficult for them to rely on God like they should.

I know this because I have experienced this. My sisters and I are strong women. We all tend to tackle problems head-on, and rarely let obstacles stand in our way. We plow through hard things, and probably take on too many projects at once. In the process, it's easy to rely on our own strength and gain a false sense of worth based on our achievements or work ethic. My sisters and I are not alone—I see this mentality in our Mennonite communities.

In a culture where weakness is considered shameful, it's hard to accept that we are made of dust. One of my favorite verses is found in Psalm 103 where King David, the great warrior, wrote:

> *"As a father has compassion on his children, so the Lord has compassion on those who fear him; for he knows how we are formed, he remembers that we are dust."*
> Psalm 103:13-14

If we consider ourselves anything other than weak, we are delusional. God knows this—it's us who need reminding.

I remember finally coming to this conclusion in my thirties when my depression was at its worst. I struggled to accomplish the simplest task and could not motivate myself to get off the couch. As I looked at my messy home with dishes piled on the counter, toys strewn in the living room, and unfolded laundry piled in the corner, I berated myself for my 'laziness'. *I should be a better mom than this. I should be a better wife than this. I am a failure.*

It was then that God whispered to my heart, "Do you think I love you based on a clean house? Do you think my love for you is only for when you are strong and competent? I remember that you are dust and that you are weak."

I was a bit stunned because I realized that, yes, I did think God's love for me was based on how well I performed as a wife and mom. If I failed, then He must be disappointed in me. If I did well, then He was pleased. My theology was clearly in need of some truth! I didn't understand that the gift of His love was not dependent on anything I could contribute. I could bring nothing to the table but my weakness and sins. Once I began to understand this, I was able to let go of my perfectionism and striving. Instead of fighting to be loved and accepted, I began to live out of His love.

Accepting our weaknesses is the first step to accepting God's strength. Once I understood that I was capable of doing *nothing* of true value on my own, I began to understand the mystery of the Christian life. I traded my weakness for His strength. My sin for His grace. My empty hands for the fullness of His Spirit.

If we are going to be the *ezer kenegdos* God created us to be, we have to acknowledge that we won't be able to do so on our own. We can only be the women God has called us to be if His Spirit lives inside of us; otherwise, we are striving for the impossible.

THE WORK OF THE SPIRIT

As a Mennonite, I did not grow up hearing about the Holy Spirit; I never heard a sermon about the Holy Spirit in all the years I attended a Mennonite church. I may have heard a few sermons on the topic when I attended an evangelical church as a teen, but even then, I did not fully comprehend what the purpose of the Holy Spirit was.

It seems that within fundamentalist circles there is a reluctance to embrace the mystery surrounding the Holy Spirit, so it's considered a subject best left untouched. I've often joked that the Mennonite theology I grew up with went something like this: Once saved, a Mennonite thanks Jesus for saving him and says, "See you in heaven, God. I've got it from here," then lives his entire life without the help of the Holy Spirit because he (or she) does not understand that the Holy Spirit is given to us as a gift.

I once heard a preacher liken this to a man who walks to work every day because he doesn't own a car. One day, he is gifted a beautiful, brand-new SUV, but because he has never learned how to drive, he leaves it sitting in his garage and continues to walk to work. If we saw that, we would likely say, "What a fool! He has been given this amazing gift for free and he doesn't use it!"

In the same way, we have been given an incredible gift, but if we don't understand how to live by the Spirit, we will never live in the fullness, intimacy, victory or power which God intended for us as believers. When Jesus ascended into heaven after His resurrection, He made a point of telling His disciples, "... it is to your advantage that I go away, for if I do not go away, the Helper will not come to you" (John 16:7, ESV).

At first, this seems preposterous. What could be better than Jesus?! How often have we said to ourselves, "If only Jesus was here." But, according to Jesus Himself, the Holy Spirit is better. Why? Because, unlike Jesus (who confined Himself to a human body prone to hunger, fatigue and illness, and limited by time and location), the Holy Spirit hovers over the earth and lives in the hearts of all believers. The same Holy Spirit who resides in me resides in you.

The Holy Spirit was given to us to help us live in the space between our salvation (which we find through Christ Jesus) and the day we reach our home in heaven with God our Father. We were never meant to live this life alone; God has not abandoned His children. Through His Holy Spirit, God has given us all we need for a godly life (2 Peter 1:3).

But choosing to live by the Spirit is just that—a choice.

While Christians are sealed by the Holy Spirit upon salvation, the ongoing goal of sanctification means we need to learn to live in full surrender to the Spirit every day of our lives. I believe part of the confusion (and reason why many Christians become disheartened is, in part, because they fail to understand the need for 'dying to self' and the sacrifices they must make to live a surrendered life. When we choose to follow Christ, we are saying, "Not my will, but yours, God. Not my life, but yours." It means getting up every morning, putting your feet on the floor, declaring, "Today I choose to follow you, God," and allowing Him to dictate your agenda. Romans 12:1 talks about this when it says we are called to be a 'living sacrifice', but as Rick Warren points out, "The problem with a living sacrifice is that it keeps crawling off the altar."[42]

Our commitment to God must be renewed day by day. Some days are easier than others. Some days our surrender is whole-hearted and joyful; other days, we struggle with our flesh and want to do things our own way. But if we long to live a life that is fruitful and at peace, we must learn to surrender again and again and again.

Another aspect of the struggle is feeling like the Christian life is an uphill battle—impossible and exhausting. If we are living in our own strength, this is true. We are limited in our ability; all our striving will never accomplish what we want it to.

Charles Price shares a story about the time he left on a business trip during the summer, which meant his wife would need to mow the lawn. She struggled to figure out how the lawnmower worked. It looked easy enough when her husband did it, but she found herself pushing with all her might to get it to move across the yard. After one round, she was exhausted and confused. How did her husband make it look so easy? While she pondered this, her fingers accidentally found the clutch and put the lawnmower into gear. Instantly, the mower moved, and soon she found herself almost running to keep up with the machine as it glided effortlessly over the lawn.[43]

This is the difference between a life lived in our own strength and a life lived in Christ.

---

[42] Rick Warren, *The Purpose Driven Life*, HarperCollins Religious US, 2014

[43] Price, C. W. *Alive in Christ: How to Find Renewed Spiritual Power*, Kregel Publications, 1995

THE SPIRIT-FILLED LIFE OF AN 'EZER KENEGDO'

You and I have been given an identity and calling straight from the Father's heart. He created us to be women who are wholly devoted to Him. As we pursue our calling, we must be mindful of our need of the Holy Spirit and acknowledge that we can do nothing apart from the Spirit at work within us. If I wish to leave a legacy of faith and godliness, it begins with me surrendering my heart and living every day in obedience to God's Word.

The beauty of obedience is that I never have to worry about its fruit—it will be there in due time. As long as I seek after God, He takes care of the outcome. What will be the fruit of a faithful life? One of my favorite examples is found in the book of Ezekiel where the prophet shares a vision given to him by an angelic guide. In chapter forty-seven we read:

> *"The man brought me back to the entrance to the temple, and I saw water coming out from under the threshold of the temple toward the east (for the temple faced east). The water was coming down from under the south side of the temple, south of the altar. He then brought me out through the north gate and led me around the outside to the outer gate facing east, and the water was trickling from the south side.*
>
> *As the man went eastward with a measuring line in his hand, he measured off a thousand cubits and then led me through water that was ankle-deep. He measured off another thousand cubits and led me through water that was knee-deep. He measured off another thousand and led me through water that was up to the waist. He measured off another thousand, but now it was a river that I could not cross, because the water had risen and was deep enough to swim in—a river that no one could cross. He asked me, 'Son of man, do you see this?'*

> *Then he led me back to the bank of the river. When I arrived there, I saw a great number of trees on each side of the river. He said to me, 'This water flows toward the eastern region and goes down into the Arabah, where it enters the Dead Sea. When it empties into the sea, the salty water there becomes fresh. Swarms of living creatures will live wherever the river flows. There will be large numbers of fish, because this water flows there and makes the salt water fresh; so where the river flows everything will live . . . Fruit trees of all kinds will grow on both banks of the river. Their leaves will not wither, nor will their fruit fail. Every month they will bear fruit, because the water from the sanctuary flows to them. Their fruit will serve for food and their leaves for healing.'"*
> *Ezekiel 47:1-9,12*

Let's take a closer look at this passage. Ezekiel describes water coming from under the temple where God resides. In other words, God is the source of this river of life. At first, the water is a trickle, but as it flows, the water becomes deeper and wider until it is "deep enough to swim in—a river that no one could cross." This river brings life wherever it goes, even to a dead sea. Creatures great and small are given nourishment from this river, and fruit trees flourish by its side.

This is what I imagine a life of obedience looks like.

At first, it may appear my life is just a trickle—nothing magical or shiny. I'm just an ordinary woman making supper for my family, paying the bills, mowing the lawn, and leading worship in church. There is nothing grand to show for my forty-some years on earth, but I am trusting my life has eternal value and that my surrender to Christ is yielding fruit.

The trickle widens to a creek, and I wonder, *what impact does my obedience have on my children?* Slowly, the creek deepens into a river. *How does my faith affect my family and my church?* As time passes and the river gets wider and disappears around the bend, I ask myself, *what impact will my obedience have on my grandchildren? In my community?*

The truth is, I may never know. I can't see that far—I can only ever see the trickle. But I can rest assured that God is using my life, my obedience and my surrender, to bless others. It may be around the bend and out of sight, but my decision to obey Christ is bringing life to someone, somewhere.

This is the promise we have when we put our lives in God's hands. He takes what we surrender and multiplies it. He uses it to bless others and glorify Himself. I don't have to worry about the outcome. I simply focus on following God's agenda and being faithful today.

YOUR LEGACY

You have a legacy too. For better or worse, you will leave a lasting impression on your children and your family. You will influence your church and community whether you are intentional or not, so ask yourself this question and give yourself time to think it through: *What kind of 'ezer kenegdo' do you want to be?*

I think we all want our lives to matter and to have eternal impact. I know I do.

We want to be like Mary sitting at Jesus' feet. We want to be teaching like Priscilla, serving like Dorcas, leading like Deborah, fighting for the innocent like Abigail, and growing in our faith like Sarah. No one wants to be a Sapphira, but the choice about who we become is made day by day in both the little decisions and the big trials.

God is calling you to Himself. He is inviting you to a journey of faith where you learn to depend on Him. He does so with the expectation that you will walk as a woman, an *ezer kenegdo*. He is not expecting you to be great. He has no false notions that you will be perfect. In fact, He already knows who you are. He knows all your complexities, sins, and failures. He sees you. He knows you. He loves you. And He invites you to partner with Him anyway.

Will you step into your calling and embrace it with all your heart? The world is a dark and chaotic place. Our families, churches and communities are desperately in need of women who are ready to pick up their cross, follow Christ, and be the *ezer kenegdos* God created us to be.

Recommended Resources

Alive in Christ: How to Find Renewed Spiritual Power
by Charles W. Price

But I Flourish: Learn to Thrive in Every Season
by Aimee Walker

Christ for Real: How to Grow in God's Likeness
by Charles W. Price

*The Making of Biblical Womanhood:
How the Subjugation of Women Became Gospel Truth*
by Beth Allison Barr

*The Wounded Heart:
Hope for Adult Victims of Childhood Sexual Abuse*
by Dr. Dan B. Allender

Worthy: Celebrating the Value of Women
by Elyse Fitzpatrick & Eric Schumacher

*Called to Peace: A Survivor's Guide to Finding
Peace & Healing After Domestic Abuse*
by Joy Forrest

*Called To Peace Ministries
(offering hope and healing to victims of domestic abuse)*
www.calledtopeace.org

Acknowledgements

Being a first-time author, I now understand the importance of this page. Having gone through the experience of writing and working with an editorial team, I have a much deeper understanding and appreciation of what it takes to write a book. It is indeed a team effort.

I am deeply indebted to Anya McKee and the team at Torn Curtain Publishing. Without their expertise, my manuscript would still be lost somewhere in my Word files. Not only did they pull together the many pieces required to produce this book, they challenged me to keep going when I wanted to burn it to the ground. Our introduction was no accident, and I thank God that He arranged our meeting.

Many thanks to my pastor, Dan Carlaw, who became a sounding board for this project in its early stages and believed in me when I was not yet certain I could pull this project together. Thank you also to Dr. Bill Taylor, Executive Director of the Evangelical Free Church of Canada, and Neil Bassingthwaighte, ServeCanada Director of the Evangelical Free Church of Canada for helping me work through the theology of this subject. Your wisdom was greatly appreciated.

What is a woman without her friends? Thank you to my sisters, Nita, Susie, and Kari, also Anna and Lara who drank multiple cups of coffee with me to discuss the real-life implications of what it means to be a 'help meet'. You are all a gift to me!

Thank you to my children, Courtney, Calum, and Cameron, who have been some of my loudest supporters and champions from the beginning. Sometimes I am amazed at their wisdom and insight and then I remember that I'm their mother.

Lastly, thank you to my husband, Jim, who has been my most faithful friend and supporter. His quiet strength has been a refuge over the years and given me courage to tackle the harder elements of my story. This book is a testimony of our years together, working to understand and support each other so we can fully step into the purpose God has for both of us. You are the best!

About the Author

Maria Dyck is a writer, speaker, and host of the *Mennonite Girls in a Modern World* podcast with a passion for helping women find freedom and healing in Christ. This is her first book.

Maria has written for several publications including *(in)courage, Fathom Magazine,* and *The Joyful Life Magazine* where she served as a blog editor and devotional writer. Her podcast is a unique look at life and faith from a Mennonite perspective and has reached women all over the world. Aside from writing, Maria has also served as a worship leader, Sunday school teacher and Bible study leader in her local church, and loves engaging in rich theological discussions with her friends.

Having lived for several years in Belize and in northern British Columbia, Maria and her husband currently make their home in northern Alberta along with their daughter and two sons. When she's not writing, you will find Maria either in her garden or tackling a new home improvement project.

If you would like to connect with her, you can reach Maria at her blog, **www.whenwallstumble.net**, email at **hello@whenwallstumble.net**, or find her on Instagram and Facebook.

www.ingramcontent.com/pod-product-compliance
Lightning Source LLC
Chambersburg PA
CBHW031251290426
44109CB00012B/526